60-DAY DEVOTIONAL

WOMAN *of* GOD

*Devotions and Prayers
to Embrace God's Call and
Fulfill His Purpose*

Candace Writes

**ROCKRIDGE
PRESS**

Copyright © 2022 by Rockridge Press

Scriptures taken from the Holy Bible, New International Version®, NIV®. Copyright © 1973, 1978, 1984, 2011 by Biblica, Inc.™ Used by permission of Zondervan. All rights reserved worldwide. www.zondervan.com. The "NIV" and "New International Version" are trademarks registered in the United States Patent and Trademark Office by Biblica, Inc.™

All rights reserved. No part of this publication may be reproduced, stored in a retrieval system, or transmitted in any form or by any means, electronic, mechanical, photocopying, recording, scanning, or otherwise, without the prior written permission of the Publisher. Requests to the Publisher for permission should be addressed to the Permissions Department, Rockridge Press, 1955 Broadway, Suite 400, Oakland, CA 94612.

First Rockridge Press trade paperback edition 2022

Rockridge Press and the Rockridge Press logo are trademarks or registered trademarks of Callisto Media Inc. and/or its affiliates in the United States and other countries and may not be used without written permission.

For general information on our other products and services, please contact our Customer Care Department within the United States at (866) 744-2665, or outside the United States at (510) 253-0500.

Paperback ISBN: 978-1-63878-717-4 | eBook ISBN: 978-1-68539-947-4

Manufactured in the United States of America

Art Director: Helen Bruno
Interior and Cover Designer: Kristina Spencer
Art Producer: Maya Melenchuk
Editor: John Makowski
Production Manager: Lanore Coloprisco

Author photo courtesy of Emma Cheshire, We Dream Photography.
Illustrations © Olga Koelsch/Creative Market.

10 9 8 7 6 5 4 3 2 1 0

I dedicate this devotional to any woman looking for or rediscovering her purpose in becoming the woman God created her to be. I pray your numerous gifts will be revealed to and reignited in you, allowing you to honor God by shining your light on others.

Contents

SECTION 2: OPENING YOUR HEART TO GOD'S PLAN   33

SECTION 3: FINDING PURPOSE IN YOUR FAITH   65

SECTION 4: WALKING THE PATH GOD HAS LAID 97

Introduction

Hey there. I'm glad you're here to embark upon this sixty-day journey with me, to strengthen your relationship with God while you're discovering His plans for your life. As women of God, we were created with purpose. In Jeremiah 1:5, God reveals, "Before I formed you in the womb, I knew you before you were born. I set you apart; I appointed you as a prophet to the nations." When God breathed life into our bodies, He also breathed purpose, setting us apart and equipping us with gifts, callings, and talents to fulfill that purpose. As we experience trials and tribulations, joys and sorrows, there are seasons where we're left wondering, "What's our purpose?" I've been there on several occasions. What I've found is that all those gifts we have been given will drive our purpose.

As a mother of two growing and energetic boys, and a minister, author, and therapist, I understand our purpose is multifaceted, ever changing, and distinctive. Spending time with God and studying His Word have encouraged, strengthened, and edified me in seeing the beauty of being aligned with His will and embracing it. I think you'll find that as you align with God's purpose for you, you'll begin to see yourself the way He does.

Please show compassion and kindness to yourself as you grow as a woman of God. There will certainly be moments when God will instantaneously speak to you through the words on these pages. Other times, you'll have to pause, reflect, and ask God to reveal what He's teaching you. That's okay. Isaiah 30:18 reads: "Yet the Lord longs to be gracious to you; therefore, he will rise

up to show you compassion, for the Lord is a God of justice. Blessed are all who wait for him." God is happily waiting for *you*, and as your sister, I have been fervently praying for you as you dig deeper into your purpose.

HOW TO USE THIS DEVOTIONAL

Before you begin reading, let's take a moment to go over how to use the *Woman of God* devotional. As we explore, meditate, and study scriptures throughout this devotional, we will use the New International Version (NIV) of the Bible. You may follow along using whichever version you like, however.

Although this devotional is not guided by date stamps, you should read it from beginning to end. I suggest you use a journal or notebook for your notes and reflections instead of only this devotional. Regardless of how you keep daily notes on the quotes and commentaries, allow God to show you their relevance in your life as you continue to evolve.

Every devotional day begins with scripture, followed by commentary, reflections, activities, and a guided prayer. You may want to set aside a specific time to sit and read the daily devotional, but remember God is leading. Yield to His voice, as at times He may want you to reflect upon a particular passage before moving on to the next page. It's not a race.

Now, let's turn the page and begin!

Accepting God's Love

In this first section, embrace God's love, knowing it is unchanging and unfailing. It is "agape love"—the highest kind of love: committed, faithful, and eternal. As you grow as a woman, embracing God's love, it's encouraging to know you can rest in your faith in God: He knows what's best for you, He will never abandon you, and He is so fond of you. There is no love greater than the love of God. And He can't wait to shower you with more.

DAY 1

Discovering Your Gifts

. . . and I have filled him with the Spirit of God, with wisdom, with understanding, with knowledge and with all kinds of skills.
—Exodus 31:3

"The two most important days in your life are the day you are born and the day you find out why" is a quote commonly attributed to humorist and novelist Mark Twain. Discovering that "why" might not be easy. We all have different reasons. But one thing we have in common is that our "whys" are to glorify God in the best way we know how.

God has given you passions that you love, and He gives you free will in how you use them. Are you using them to worship Him and advance His kingdom? Sitting down with yourself to figure out what you're passionate about, skilled at, and enjoy doing will help you figure out your purpose. Putting those passions to serve God is your purpose.

Tabitha is a fantastic example of how to make the most of your resources. Tabitha is described in Acts 9:36 as a disciple who is always doing good for others, helping the needy and offering her time and resources. Tabitha was described as a follower of Christ because her life displayed His love in how she cared for and was motivated to help others. Tabitha's faith touched many who lived in Lydda, and her character showed care and compassion. Others were drawn to Tabitha's life and impact because they wanted to know more about the God she served. She was a witness to many. God wants to use you in this way as well.

REFLECTION

- How can you delve further into your passions to find or fulfill your purpose?

- Which of your gifts are you currently using to advance God's Kingdom?

ACTIVITY

Make a list of gifts you are passionate about. Think of ways you can use them to honor God. What actions can you implement or perform today? This week?

GUIDED PRAYER

God, I return my gifts to You. Please help me identify ways to use what You've given me to positively impact others in my sphere of influence. Amen.

Quality Time

The Lord is near to all who call on him,
to all who call on him in truth.

—Psalm 145:18

God is eager to learn more about the woman you have become so that He can disclose His plans, ideas, and answered prayers to you. God is saying, "I want more of you," "I'm looking forward to your company," and "I want to know more about you and your thoughts." God loves spending quality time with you.

God also desires that you learn more about Him. There's intimacy when you spend one-on-one time with someone. Intimacy can be defined as "into-me-you-see," as some aspects of God are revealed only in this space. Being in God's presence allows you to learn His qualities, and being close to Him is incredibly fulfilling.

Sitting down with your Bible open is not the only way to converse with God. There are many options. If you enjoy painting, for example, transform it into a form of praise by painting while listening to worship music. If you enjoy nature, pray aloud while hiking. Even if you have a busy schedule, you can make time for God by praising Him in the car, in the shower, or while preparing meals. He is everywhere and in everything; all we need to do is say hello.

Just as you spend time with others, think about greeting God as you go about your day. Taking time to learn about Him will help you understand your purpose and grow into the woman God created you to be.

REFLECTION

- Where and when will you set aside time for God today? Tomorrow? On a regular basis?

- How do you enjoy spending time with God the most?

ACTIVITY

During your most menial chores today (sitting in traffic, doing the dishes), strike up a conversation with God. Let Him know how happy you are to be refocused on your journey. Listen to, and write down, what He has to say.

GUIDED PRAYER

God, I want to spend more time in Your presence because I love You. Please help me make more room for You to live freely in my life. Amen.

For God So Loved the World

> For God so loved the world that he gave his one and only Son, that whoever believes in him shall not perish but have eternal life. For God did not send his Son into the world to condemn the world, but to save the world through him.
>
> —John 3:16-17

John 3:16 is a well-known Bible verse. It is one of the first verses most Christians learn when developing a relationship with God. It's indescribable that God sent His one and only Son as an act of love to save us, so that we will have eternal life. Can you imagine willingly handing over your son, or any beloved family member, knowing they are going to be put to death? Or being the one who's willingly handing themselves over, knowing what's coming? It's inconceivable. When I think about what happened on Calvary that day, as Jesus hung His head and died for our sins, I am so humbled that he paid the ultimate price for *me*. For *you*. Words fail me, because there are none that could fully express the magnitude of love that He would lay down His own life so that we could live.

Jesus understood His purpose in the world. He humanly felt all emotions and surely grew tired of betrayal, loss, deception, and envy—yet still he chose to die for us. He fulfilled His purpose.

We can show our love when we live good lives, when we follow God's will for our lives, and when we discover our purpose by saying yes to Him. In our faith journey, we work to ensure everything we touch and accomplish will bring glory to His name. That's how we say thank you.

REFLECTION

- When you think about John 3:16–17, what thoughts or feelings come to mind?

- God's love is unfailing; how do you define unfailing love?

ACTIVITY

As you ponder what happened on Calvary, draw a heart in your journal and write all the words that describe Jesus's selfless act of love inside it.

GUIDED PRAYER

God, there are no adequate words to express Your love for me. Still, I give You my life and will spend my days seeking Your will for my life, to bring glory to Your name. Amen.

God's Love Is Unparalleled

"My son," the father said, "you are always with me, and everything I have is yours. But we had to celebrate and be glad, because this brother of yours was dead and is alive again: he was lost and is found."

—*Luke 15:31–32*

To offer a quick overview, today's verse is about the prodigal son. It's a story about two sons who inherited their father's fortune. The younger went off and mistreated his blessing, and when he came to his senses (and was out of money), he returned home. In verse 20, it reads, "So he got up and went to his father. But while he was still a long way off, his father saw him and was filled with compassion for him; he ran to his son, threw his arms around him, and kissed him." His father hugged him warmly, because his love for his son never wavered. The father rejoiced in his son's homecoming (the present) instead of focusing on his poor choices (the past).

It's much like God's great love for us. He loves us so profoundly that we, like the prodigal son, can always come home to open arms. God's love is unparalleled and always available.

God demonstrates His love for us in so many ways that naming just one is difficult. When I think about God's love, I remember how He loved me even when I did not love myself. He hung on to me even when I wanted to give up. Even when I went astray, seeking to live life on my own terms, God was there, covering, protecting, and loving me in the midst of it all. I see myself in the prodigal son. Join me in gratefully accepting God's forgiveness and love.

REFLECTION

- What thoughts come to mind when you consider God's love for you?

- How has God recently demonstrated His love through His actions?

ACTIVITY

After reflecting on God's unchanging love, read Luke 15:11–32. Write your thoughts on it in your journal. What is it telling you right now?

GUIDED PRAYER

God, thank You for loving and covering me. Thank You for demonstrating the meaning of love to me. Amen.

God Will Take Care of You

Therefore I tell you, do not worry about your life, what you will eat or drink; or about your body, what you will wear. Is not life more than food, and the body more than clothes? Look at the birds of the air; they do not sow or reap or store away in barns, and yet your heavenly Father feeds them. Are you not much more valuable than they?
—Matthew 6:25–26

One morning, I was lying in bed, listening to the birds chirping outside my window, when Matthew 6:25–26 came to mind. I thought about how happy the birds sounded and how God cares for them by feeding them. The night before, I couldn't help but stay up late thinking about what was going on in my life that was causing me to worry and, at times, panic. Now, the next morning, as I listened to the birds, I heard God whispering, "Don't be alarmed. You can count on Me." I remembered how much God loves me, and how He cares for me even more than those happy birds.

God's love for us is evident in His grace, mercy, care, and concern for our needs. Philippians 4:19 says, "And my God will meet all your needs according to the riches of his glory in Christ Jesus." We are all human, and we all feel anxious at times, especially when there is a lot of uncertainty. Even so, God loves us. We might not always see or understand it in the moment, but God has things under control.

God is Jehovah Jireh, our Provider, and He will not withhold anything good from us. Consider yourself His favorite because God is constantly watching out for you, just as He is for the joyous chirping and soaring birds in the sky.

REFLECTION

- After reading today's devotion, what comes to mind about God always showing up and making sure you have everything you need?

- How did God speak to you after reading Matthew 6:25–26?

ACTIVITY

It's time to give God your anxieties and other things that deprive you of peace and rest, believing that He will take care of you. Make a list of the areas of your life that are causing you concern. Pray over them and release them to God. Then stop worrying. God will handle it.

GUIDED PRAYER

God, I love You. Thank You for caring about me and providing for me. I am forever grateful. Please help me feel Your strength and let me let go of my worries. Amen.

DAY 6

God Is Love

*Love is patient, love is kind. It does not envy, it does
not boast, it is not proud. It does not dishonor others,
it is not self-seeking, it is not easily angered, it keeps
no record of wrongs. Love does not delight in evil but
rejoices with the truth. It always protects, always trusts,
always hopes, always perseveres.*
—1 Corinthians 13:4–7

God commands us to love one another, and as you evolve as a woman aligning your life with God's plan, you will encounter many situations in which love should be your answer. You might ask, "What does this entail? How is love the answer?" I am so glad you asked. I will tell you a story.

I spoke with a couple who had been married for twenty years, to discuss forgiveness and their love for one another. One of the lessons the woman taught me was basically: If I can't forgive my spouse, how can I ask God to forgive me? God entrusted us with one another, and it is exhausting to keep a record of the number of times we miss the mark. I am patient in this love because God has been patient with me. I am kind in this love because God is kind to me. I forgive in this love because God hasn't stopped and will not stop forgiving me. God's love has shown me how to love.

I still think about her words regularly. I am sharing them with you because they're a great example of understanding how God is our first model of love. No matter the circumstance, we should still love, and show up with and in love, whether romantic love, platonic love, or love extended to our neighbor.

REFLECTION

- Are you in alignment with 1 Corinthians 13:4–7? If so, what part have you mastered? If not, what parts of the scripture do you need to work on right now?

- What comes to mind when you think of love? It can be spiritual, practical, or a memory. What words do you use to describe God's love for you? For others?

ACTIVITY

Write a letter to God thanking Him for His love, or write down the lyrics to a song that reminds you of God's great love.

GUIDED PRAYER

God, You have shown me the true meaning of love by giving me Yours, the best version of love. Please help me love as You've modeled, and assist me in being kind, forgiving, and patient. Amen.

The Potter's Hand

Yet you, Lord, are our Father. We are the clay, you are the potter; we are all the work of your hand.
—Isaiah 64:8

I enjoy molding and constructing with playdough and especially did as a child. There are, however, distinct differences between the clay I play with and the kind used by, say, a company that makes and sells pottery. The main difference is that I use water-based clay, whereas the pros use oil-based clay. Their clay holds its shape longer; mine is best for temporary creations.

Think of the process oil itself undergoes in its creation: the pressing to keep only goodness and the value of it in its final form. Similarly, in accepting God's love, you trust Him to continually refine and prepare you for greatness. When He's involved, it's long-lasting and substantial, as God completes what He begins. In Him we are solidly cared for and nurtured.

God is the Master Potter, looking into our hearts as we live, pruning anything crooked, and straightening our paths. Psalm 16:11 says, "You make known to me the path of life; you will fill me with joy in your presence, with eternal pleasures at your right hand."

As you reflect on your life, can you say that you are teachable, willing to receive God's molding, and willing to let go of people, places, or things that do not align with your purpose? God is a master at shaping and preparing us for the good future He promised, but we must first allow Him to do so. How else can we walk the path created for us?

REFLECTION

- After reading today's devotion, what thoughts came to your mind?

- What areas of your life has God refined and molded for His glory?

ACTIVITY

Reflect on and list the social engagements and activities you currently participate in. Are they appropriate for who you are now? Write down ways to phase out those that aren't.

GUIDED PRAYER

God, give me the wisdom to let go of things that no longer serve a purpose. Help me believe in the process and keep my eyes on Your promise. Amen.

Receiving God's Correction

> Those whom I love I rebuke and discipline.
> So be earnest and repent.
> —*Revelation 3:19*

My four-year-old son, Braxton, was given an electric toy 4x4 on Christmas morning. He was so ecstatic about the gift that he wanted to drive it right away. I told him that going on the street was dangerous, so he should stay on the sidewalk or the grass. He looked displeased with my request but softly said, "Okay, Mommy." He followed my directions briefly, and then turned sharply into our neighborhood parking lot. I dashed in front of his little truck and motioned for him to stop.

Braxton did not see any trouble with his choice. I, however, noticed potholes and careless drivers, and my love for Braxton will always seek to protect him; I see what he does not see. Braxton, I'm sure, didn't share my sentiments, thinking, *My mommy is interfering with my enjoyment.* After I corrected and steered Braxton to safety, I pondered how often we believe God is interfering in our life because we think we know ourselves better than God does.

When you love someone, you will disrupt their flow to ensure they are not subjected to harm, hurt, or danger. When you open your heart to be responsive to God's purpose and pray, "Lord, protect me," He'll step in just like a good Father. We can freely flow in His will when we are teachable and open to receiving God's correction as a form of love, rather than chastisement.

There will be bumps in the road, but if God is with us, those obstacles will not derail us.

REFLECTION

- What do you think of when you hear the term "discipline"? Do you think it's a bad thing? If so, why?

- How do you deal with correction in your interpersonal connections, such as with your children, nieces/nephews, students, and coworkers?

ACTIVITY

Write down constructive and positive ways to tell someone "No, that's not right," "You can't do that," and "You have to stop that behavior" that allow your care and love to shine through.

GUIDED PRAYER

God, thank You for correcting me. I accept it as a sign of Your love, and I think it's intended to help me grow, develop, and align with my purpose. Amen.

DAY 9

More Than Enough

Now to him who is able to do immeasurably more than all we ask or imagine, according to his power that is at work within us.
—*Ephesians 3:20*

I believe I'm a patient person. One time, in the thick of the pandemic, I ordered two T-shirts from an online boutique. Weeks passed, then months, and my package was still missing. I contacted the company about my shirts never being delivered. They were very kind, offering me an additional item free of charge due to the delay, so I added a sweater. I waited even longer the second time around, but I never complained.

When the box arrived, I was surprised to find that along with the other items, I received a hat and a mask. When I noticed the extra items, Ephesians 3:20 came to mind, and I smiled. I reflected on how many times God has used adversity in my life to turn around and honor my response by providing me with more than I expected.

Every action we take as women of God serves a purpose. We are living examples of God's mercy, grace, and compassion. God's love resides within us, and how we choose to treat others and behave when things don't go as planned reflects that love. I believe God watched how I responded. I could have been an angry customer and belittled the salesperson or barraged the internet with low store ratings, but I didn't. I was patient. I responded patiently, and when you dwell in God's love, He honors you by providing more than enough.

REFLECTION

- When was the last time something in your life did not go as planned, and how did you handle it?

- How would you have handled a situation similar to the one described in today's devotion?

ACTIVITY

Read Galatians 5:22–23 and write down what God reveals to you in this passage of scripture.

GUIDED PRAYER

God, when things don't go as planned, I want to respond to others with love, grace, and kindness. Please assist me in this area of my life. Amen.

Don't Question God?

If any of you lacks wisdom, you should ask God,
who gives generously to all without finding fault,
and it will be given to you.

—James 1:5

When tragedy or uncertainty arise, you've probably heard the phrase "Don't question God." But I learned it's entirely reasonable to ask God questions. He actually welcomes it. Conversing with God and questioning Him are in fact necessary for navigating life and identifying your purpose.

There are numerous stories in the Bible in which people seek guidance. For example, the prophet Habakkuk was struggling to figure out why God allowed the people of Israel to face such hardship. In Habakkuk 1:2–3, he says, "How long, Lord, must I call for help, but you do not listen? Or cry out to you, 'Violence!' but you do not save? Why do you make me look at injustice? Why do you tolerate wrong-doing?" The Lord responds to Habakkuk, beginning in verse 5, stating, "Look at the nations and watch—and be utterly amazed. For I am going to do something in your days that you would not believe, even if you were told."

God did not provide a complete description of His work behind the scenes, yet He provided Habakkuk with reassurance, comfort, and hope. God assured him that even amid difficulty, He has everything under control.

It's acceptable for us to ask God questions, too. Not sure where your journey is heading? Pray to God. Having trouble as you seek your purpose? Turn to God. He is always inclined and willing to answer.

REFLECTION

- What are your thoughts regarding the statement "Don't question God"? Has your perspective changed since you were young?

- When was the last time you asked God a question? Does it bring you peace or comfort knowing that it's alright to ask your questions?

ACTIVITY

Grab your journal. Write down questions for God, one per page. Write down God's answer to each as soon as He responds. Are the answers what you were hoping or expecting? Did they come earlier or later than you expected?

GUIDED PRAYER

God, thank You for being so kind to me in my time of need, being willing to sit with me, and providing me with the answers I need. Amen.

You Are Not Your Past

Therefore, if anyone is in Christ, the new creation has come: The old has gone, the new is here!
—*2 Corinthians 5:17*

At one point in her life, my friend Andrea dealt with feelings of guilt and shame related to failed relationships and missed opportunities. One day, she reached out to me, telling me that she was still dealing with old wounds and couldn't fully step into her purpose. She also shared that God was opening numerous doors in her career, propelling her from one level to the next, and she didn't feel deserving of His goodness. As I watched God extend His grace to her, I thought about how we all have a past. But our history does not define us, nor does it influence the future He has in store for us. God wants to shower us with His goodness. Let Him!

It makes no difference what others think—because God has the final say in everything that happens in our lives. When you look to God and keep your eyes fixed on Him, He will direct your steps, and your future will appear brighter than your past. You must first let go, however. Let Him lead. There's a lot God wants to accomplish through you. If anything keeps you tied down, whether intellectually, emotionally, or physically, God wants to remove the obstruction so that your path ahead is clear. You are not a product of your past, and you are not your mistakes.

In order to fully step into your purpose, you must let go, forgive, heal, move forward, and begin to walk confidently in your purpose. Each day is a new opportunity to glorify God's name—and for Him to celebrate you.

REFLECTION

- List at least two things that happened in the past that you need to break free from.

- Is there anything preventing you from truly embracing God's plan for your life?

ACTIVITY

Write a farewell letter to your past. Identify the roadblocks and circumstances that kept you stuck in a cycle and what you hope to experience in the future. Then write a prayer to God, asking Him to guide you as you move forward with a renewed mind.

GUIDED PRAYER

Please, God, help me release events from my past that prevent me from feeling confident and unsure of my purpose. Please help me understand my past does not dictate my future. Amen.

The Courage to Speak

For if you remain silent at this time, relief and
deliverance for the Jews will arise from another place,
but you and your father's family will perish. And who
knows but that you have come to your royal position for
such a time as this?

—*Esther 4:14*

Some four hundred years before Christ, there was Esther, a Jewish orphan looked after by her cousin Mordecai. Her story begins with King Xerxes of Persia searching for a new queen after Queen Vashti disobeyed him. He invited all Persia's virgin women to the palace so he could choose a new queen from among them. Mordecai warned Esther not to divulge that she was Jewish because Jews were shunned and treated as second-class citizens. When the women were presented to King Xerxes, he chose Esther as his new queen.

While Esther was residing in the palace, one of the palace's attendants informed her that King Xerxes's second-in-command was scheming to destroy the Jewish people of Persia. Esther was afraid to approach the king. Mordecai asked her, "What if you were placed in the palace for such a time as this?" Esther bravely addressed King Xerxes, interfering with the plot and putting an end to the scheme. She courageously saved her people from destruction.

We find the strength to accomplish what's needed by turning to God. When fear creeps in, remind yourself that you are purposed for this journey, called to this journey, and graced for the journey ahead.

REFLECTION

- How has God spoken to you in the past, and how does God speak to you today?

- Can you think of a time when you were scared but God intervened and gave you the strength to act or speak up?

ACTIVITY

Today, read the Book of Esther. Did you notice there is no direct mention of God in any of the ten chapters? It's the only book of the Bible that doesn't mention God directly. Of course, that doesn't mean He's not there. Find and write down places/instances you can see God behind the scenes.

GUIDED PRAYER

God, it's a privilege to be connected to You. Extend courage to me when I'm afraid. Extend Your strength to me when I'm weak. Please help me heed to the path You've chosen for me. Amen.

Roller-Coaster Ride

Even though I walk through the darkest valley, I will fear
no evil, for you are with me; your rod and your staff, they
comfort me.
—*Psalm 23:4*

Riding on roller coasters is one of my favorite things to
do. I like the ones that travel through dark surroundings
before the passage opens and you burst into light. I was
thinking about moments with my fourteen-year-old son,
Bryson, and us riding together. He was initially interested
in going on the rides, but he didn't like his "stomach
dropping." He especially disliked roller coasters that
began in tunnels or dark areas.

One summer at a big park, everyone in our group
wanted to go on a ride similar to what I described. Bryson
was cautious at first, but he insisted on getting on the
ride. He took a seat by me, and I assured him, "Hold my
hand. I'm here with you, and there will be lights all around
us, even if it's dark. You will not be in complete darkness."
Afterward, he wanted to ride it again! He enjoyed it more
than he anticipated.

A light must be present for a shadow to appear in
the darkness. God—our Light—is with us wherever we go,
wherever He sends us. Even when you encounter difficulties, know that soon you'll be reflecting on the time when
it terrified you, but now you're loving it, eager, and willing.
Just like Bryson, you'll remember how God didn't send
you His light—because it is always present.

REFLECTION

- How can you apply today's devotion to your life?

- Can you think of a moment when you were hesitant to undertake something but are now fearless and confident with God's help?

ACTIVITY

Take part in or sign up for a fun, adventurous, and exciting activity today.

GUIDED PRAYER

God, please assist me in facing my fears and knowing You're with me at all times. Help me see the road ahead of me in a new light, accepting the challenges and joy. Amen.

DAY 14

Simon Says "Jump"

Now if you obey me fully and keep my covenant, then out of all nations you will be my treasured possession. Although the whole earth is mine . . .

—**Exodus 19:5**

Simon Says is a popular children's game. One person plays Simon and gives orders, and the others must follow their commands. For example, if Simon says, "Simon says 'Jump up and down,'" you jump up and down. If Simon does not say "Simon says" before issuing a command, such as "Touch the ground," and you follow it, you are out.

People will try to play Simon in your life. They will advise you on what you should and should not do. Someone might have come to your mind, as we've all met a Simon. There comes a time, however, when you must break free from other people's opinions and tune out their voices.

Not everyone connected to you will understand the path God is leading you down, because He gave you the vision for your path. Genesis 7 details the familiar story of Noah's Ark. In verses 1 and 2, it reads, "The Lord then said to Noah, 'Go into the ark, you and your whole family, because I have found you righteous in this generation. Take with you seven pairs of every kind of clean animal, a male and its mate . . . '" Noah followed God's command, and I am sure people thought his actions were outlandish—until the flood came.

God's actions do not always make sense to the human mind. Remember that His thoughts are not our thoughts, nor are His ways our ways. Using discernment, let God be your Simon.

REFLECTION

- Who comes to mind when you think of the Simon(s) in your life?

- When God gives you ideas, do you overshare information or do you share with wisdom?

ACTIVITY

In your journal, write out your interpretation of keeping God's covenant.

GUIDED PRAYER

God, please help me drown out the words of people who do not align with my vision. Grant me wisdom to see what You are saying and to go where You are leading. Amen.

DAY 15

The Well

Jesus answered her, "If you knew the gift of God and who it is that asks you for a drink, you would have asked him and he would have given you living water."

—John 4:10

In John 4, a Samaritan woman is getting water from her local well. There was a lot of animosity between Samaritans and Jews at this time. They tried their best to avoid one another by taking longer routes to avoid entering the other's territory when traveling.

Jesus could have taken the longer route and gone through Perea, but He insisted on traveling through Samaria because purpose was attached to this route: the woman at the well. When He asked for a drink, she couldn't understand why a man, especially a Jew, would talk to a woman. (At this time, not only did these two groups of people despise one another, but Jewish men weren't supposed speak to women in public.)

The story finishes with Jesus telling the woman that He is aware of her history of having several husbands (something people of that time would disagree with), but He is unconcerned about it. His intention was not only to fill the void in her heart but also to offer her the gift of eternal life, salvation. Jesus did not distance Himself from her because of her gender, social background, or past. Jesus went out of His way to show her His love. The woman at the well then fulfills her purpose; she went into town and evangelized after her encounter with Jesus, telling others about Him. Sharing Jesus with others is what it's all about.

REFLECTION

- Have you or someone you know been ostracized because of gender or socioeconomic standing? How has God aided you in navigating that period of your life? Or, how can you help someone in this situation?

- When was the last time you shared God's good news with someone?

ACTIVITY

What has God revealed to you about approaching people who are different from what you are used to?

GUIDED PRAYER

God, thank You for looking beyond my faults and seeing my needs. I will share my story with others to draw them near to you. Amen.

Opening Your Heart to God's Plan

In this section, you will open your heart to God's plan as you grow and align yourself with His will. Jeremiah 29:11 reads, "'For I know the plans I have for you,' declares the LORD, 'plans to prosper you and not harm you, plans to give you hope and a future.'" As you open up your heart to God, He'll sit with you to nourish your mind, body, and spirit by revealing His plan.

You're More Than Enough

Many women do noble things, but you surpass them all.
—*Proverbs 31:29*

If you read this Proverb in its entirety, you would think, *Whew, becoming this woman, is it even possible*? I asked myself this question when I first started studying Proverbs 31. I'd like us to think about the woman portrayed here as an example of traits to strive toward as we journey through life.

Some women are inspired by the woman portrayed in Proverbs 31, whereas others find her exhausting. Galatians 6:9 says, "Let us not become weary in doing good, for at the proper time we will reap a harvest if we do not give up." This is one of my favorite verses because we all become tired, but we can't give up. Before our feet even touch the ground, we're already thinking about the thousand tasks we need to complete for the day. As I think about my daily hassles, the ripping and the running, I often recall the Proverbs 31 woman.

She was committed to her own physical, emotional, and spiritual well-being. She knew her worth. As Proverbs 31:10 mentions, "She is worth far more than rubies." We're all a work in progress, but we're the women God created us to be. We too are worth more than rubies.

Many people will focus on the woman as a wife, a caregiver, an early riser, a good steward of her gifts, etc. I want us, however, to look at her as a woman who, yes, was all the things mentioned, but, most important, had an intimate relationship with God.

REFLECTION

- What is your take on the woman in Proverbs 31?

- Do you have a new perspective on her after reading today's devotion?

ACTIVITY

Look at yourself in the mirror as you say to yourself, *You are a woman of God. You deserve God's love. You are worthy.*

GUIDED PRAYER

God, please be patient as You remind me time again that it is not my works that are of value, but that I am doing them in Your name. Amen.

Making Room in Your Heart

I pray that out of his glorious riches he may strengthen you with power through his Spirit in your inner being, so that Christ may dwell in your hearts through faith. And I pray that you, being rooted and established in love, may have power, together with all the Lord's holy people, to grasp how wide and long and high and deep is the love of Christ.

—*Ephesians 3:16-18*

Having a pretty busy schedule during the week, I typically clean on Saturday mornings. There I was on the kitchen floor, looking at the challenge of a stuffed refrigerator. I grabbed trash bags and disinfectant wipes as I began to make room for fresh fruit, vegetables, and all the goodies my household enjoys.

A few moments later, I looked into a clean and spacious refrigerator where the only things left could be nourishing to our bodies. I saw I now had space for more.

I share this because God is looking to come in and overflow your heart with His fresh thoughts and give you a vision only you can fulfill. You first will have to make room in your heart for Him to accomplish this, however. To do this, start by taking inventory of your life, noting any person, place, or thing that no longer serves you or is not healthy for your mind, body, or soul. Just as I took a moment to assess what was in my refrigerator to discard or keep, we can take a moment to do the same with the people and things in our lives. By doing so, we can watch God dwell in the newly opened parts of our hearts. We allow Him to fill us with only the best of what we need to succeed.

REFLECTION

- Being reminded of God's goodness, in what ways has God blessed you by removing people, places, or things from your life?

- What is your takeaway from today's devotion, and how can you apply it to your life today?

ACTIVITY

Look at your calendar today. What can you cut out that no longer serves you and God? If there are tasks you dislike but can't avoid, can you offer them up to God while you do them?

GUIDED PRAYER

God, allow me to release what no longer serves me to make room for new opportunities and people aligned with my purpose to enter into my life. I trust that something greater is coming, and as I make room in my heart, extend to me peace and strength. Amen.

Operating Out of a Limiting Belief

Taking the five loaves and the two fish and looking up to heaven, he gave thanks and broke them. Then he gave them to the disciples to distribute to the people. They all ate and were satisfied, and the disciples picked up twelve basketfuls of broken pieces that were left over.
—Luke 9:16-17

My best friend, Monet, is a National Board–certified teacher who received her master's degree in education. She believes her purpose is to help parents of children with autism navigate through the processes within the school system.

Monet and I were on the phone one day. I asked her, "Why haven't you started your business?" She responded, "I'm procrastinating. I believe I need to be more established financially to succeed. I also need to share publicly more about my goals for people to take advice from me. Ultimately, I doubt myself."

I shared with her that she just has to trust herself and God's voice inside her. God would not give her this vision to lie dormant. At the scene of the loaves and fishes miracle, the disciples surely felt inadequate knowing they did not have the supply to meet the demand of the people. Yet they succeeded. Like the disciples, if you turn over the little you have now to God, He'll take it and release an abundance of resources—just as He did for the five thousand. You don't have to figure out how. God will.

REFLECTION

- What is your limiting belief? Is it fear, self-sabotage, doubt?

- What vision has God given you to fulfill that you are not executing because you're allowing your limiting belief to keep you in mental bondage?

ACTIVITY

Analyze the resources and tools you presently have (such as materials, subject matter experts, resources), and assess how you can create an action plan to execute your vision. The seemingly impossible hurdles? Turn them over to God.

GUIDED PRAYER

Thank You, God, for abundantly meeting my needs. I release doubt and trust that I have what I need to succeed. I pray for divine instructions as I step out of fear and into purpose. Amen.

Wrestling with a Troubled Heart

Do not let your hearts be troubled. You believe
in God; believe also in me.
—**John 14:1**

You may currently be in a season where it seems you are serving everyone's purpose but your own, causing you to become discouraged. As a result, you may have begun wrestling with despair and become unyielding to God's plan for your life.

God is always with us, ready, waiting, and willing to love on and redirect us. Hebrews 13:5 says, "Never will I leave you; never will I forsake you." When God said "never," He spoke in absolutes, which means it is not up for debate. In this season, allow God to reframe your narrative and redirect your focus, yielding to His plan for your life. He's never leaving you. He knew you would be here at this place in your life. As you continue to seek God, I hope you begin opening your heart to His plan for your life and trusting that the future predestined for you is good.

The trials and tribulations you have experienced do not define who you are, but God is so good that He'll use them for *your* good. God doesn't change His mind about us even when we change and go astray. Trust in God and open up your heart to Him, because God is concerned about you and you can be honest with Him. Tell God what is on your heart. He truly cares. Allow God's voice to penetrate your heart, since hope and goodness are already yours.

REFLECTION

- As you read today's devotion, what thoughts came to your mind?

- How are you opening yourself to God's plan for your life? Have circumstances of despair prevented you from fulfilling your purpose?

ACTIVITY

Grab your journal and complete this prompt: What do I owe myself in this season of my life? What do I need to release to open up my heart to God?

GUIDED PRAYER

God, You have never left me, and I'm grateful. As I seek You, I open my heart to discover my purpose and trust Your plan. I want to glorify You. God, guide me. Amen.

Tell the Story

Though he slay me, yet will I hope in him; I will surely defend my ways to his face.

—Job 13:15

Job was a man of integrity, self-discipline, and faithfulness to God, yet he was relentlessly tormented, from losing his livestock and children to having his house collapse. But instead of blaming God, he praised Him, and God blessed Job with more than he had previously.

This story shows us we don't all find our calling while strolling through a field of roses, lilies, and sunflowers. I was reading and meditating on the Book of Job one day when I was reminded of my sister, Aniya. She had gone through a period of suffering, as Job did, and God had kept her in the midst of it all.

She sprang to mind because she had been through a lot, including a miscarriage that necessitated many hospitalizations. Yet despite her agony and weakened voice and body, she kept believing. I was struck by her faith. Aniya worshiped God in her distress because she believed she would be healed and that her current situation would not last forever. According to Aniya, "My pain had the opportunity to meet my purpose, and my purpose arose."

Today, I weaved my sister's and Job's stories together since we've all been through painful situations, but we're still here to share God's good news. Every experience, whether pleasant or unpleasant, is connected to our purpose. As a result, realize that God will use anything you have gone through to encourage, edify, and strengthen others on their journeys. Share your story as you survived to tell it.

REFLECTION

- What comes to mind when you think about a distressing experience you overcame?

- Has God used a distressing situation for your good?

ACTIVITY

In your journal, reframe a past distress as a time God was strengthening your faith. Write down in detail how you came out stronger.

GUIDED PRAYER

God, thank You for Your grace and mercy. Thank You for allowing me to persevere in the face of adversity, knowing that everything would work out for my good. Amen.

There's Purpose While You Wait

But as for me, I watch in hope for the Lord, I wait for God my Savior; my God will hear me.
—**Micah 7:7**

On a rainy Sunday afternoon, at a small coffee shop, I sat down with a friend. Before the conversation began, her manner alerted me something was deeply bothering her. As she spoke, tears streamed down her face. "What's wrong with me?" she cried. "I am thirty-six. I am not married, I desire children, and I'm feeling the pressure of my biological clock ticking. I'm excelling as a nurse, but I feel hopeless. I should be married by now."

I silently prayed, "God, how do I comfort, reassure, and support my friend? How do I tell her Your plan for her life is good, and Your timing is perfect?" God led me to today's verse, Micah 7:7. My friend realized she has purpose at every point in her life, even while waiting for more. Our meeting on that rainy Sunday afternoon was a few years ago. Now my friend is in a loving marriage with children.

I share my friend's story to encourage you not to give up on your "now," because the amazing part about your trail is it's handcrafted by God for only you to blaze. In one season, your purpose may be to act as a gentle encourager when your coworker experiences burnout. Another season, your purpose may be running around the house, pouring into your family your time, love, and nurturing spirit. God's purpose for you is multifaceted. Isn't that wonderful? There's always a purpose for you, then, now, and in the future.

REFLECTION

- Today's devotion showed God's purpose for our lives always prevailing. In what ways were you encouraged to seek purpose while waiting?

- Are you wrestling with identifying your purpose while experiencing a waiting season? If so, what is God showing you through this devotion that you can apply to your life?

ACTIVITY

A vision board is a collection of images and words helping you visualize your dreams. For our devotion today, I want to rename it a "purpose board." Gather magazines, scissors, glue, and a marker. As God leads, create a purpose board. Use it as daily inspiration.

GUIDED PRAYER

God, I come to You with gratitude. I thank You for purpose. I believe Your timing is perfect and good. Your purpose will prevail. Amen.

The Wandering and Barren Heart

In a desert land he found him, in a barren and howling waste. He shielded him and cared for him; he guarded him as the apple of his eye.

—**Deuteronomy 32:10**

I had dinner with my friends Darius and Andrea one evening to catch up on what's happening in one another's lives. Darius is in his forties, single with no children, and works for a corporate organization. Andrea is married with four children and owns a salon. As we talked over dinner, Darius confided about being lost.

He expressed, "I'm just going through the motions right now. From the outside, I am successful. I have an excellent job, home, family, and friends, but honestly, I have been feeling hopeless, worthless, and lonely." Andrea and I looked at each other, as it confirmed what we already knew: Our friend was hurting. Darius just lost someone close to him, and his grief seemed unbearable. We had scheduled the dinner because we noticed the behavioral change in Darius.

Darius (wrongly) felt he wandered in the desert alone. But in this season, his purpose was to rest, allowing God to shield, guard, and care for him. He doesn't have to be on the mountaintop, exceeding his goals, making everyone laugh with his witty jokes all the time. There's purpose in resting. If grief seems too much, more than prayer alone can ease, God provides outside help to cope during those dark times.

REFLECTION

- Today's devotion discussed our purpose going beyond the execution of tasks. At times, it's to rest. How do you define "rest"?

- Is rest easy for you? Why or why not?

ACTIVITY

How can you incorporate more rest into your life? Jot down a self-care routine that you can integrate into your daily schedule. Then schedule a rest-centered activity for today that brings you peace and comfort.

GUIDED PRAYER

God, Help me create moments of ease in my life. Guard my heart and mind—shield and care for me as I rest to elevate my mood and regulate my emotions. I need more of You today. Amen.

Asking, Seeking, and Knocking

Ask and it will be given to you; seek and you will find; knock and the door will be opened to you.
—Matthew 7:7

One day, I was scrolling on Instagram and stumbled across a post that caught my attention. The post stated, "What's the most challenging for you to do, say 'I love you,' ask for help, or apologize?" It caused me to reflect upon a characteristic of my younger son, Braxton.

Braxton is four years old, desires autonomy, and asks for help only after trying to figure it out on his own. One night as we were going through our bedtime routine, I asked him if he needed help putting on his favorite pajamas. He said, "No, Mommy. I got this." I stepped away. After a few moments of watching him struggle, I gently asked him, "Braxton, do you need help?" He gave me the same response as I watched his shirt hang off his head. It was stuck. Then he grew weary, overwhelmed, and frustrated, beginning to cry. "Mommy, can you help me now, please?" As I helped him, he released a big sigh of relief as I got his shirt on properly.

As I laid Braxton down for bed, turning off the lights, I looked at him, pondering how many times God watches us, waiting to help, knowing all we have to do is seek His face and ask, and He's standing by with an answer. God wants you to open up your heart in receiving support to fulfill your purpose. For this reason, remember it's okay to ask for help.

REFLECTION

- Do you find it challenging to ask for help?

- In what ways is God speaking to you in this season of your life about receiving help?

ACTIVITY

What do you need help with but are afraid to ask? Maybe you have a list of chores you just can't get to, or aren't capable of doing alone. Maybe's it's a deeper set of self-help issues. Make a list of five things. Today, humbly ask someone for help with at least one of them.

GUIDED PRAYER

God, You have connected me with persons to help me carry out my purpose. I'm glad that I don't have to do life alone. Thank You. Amen.

The Beauty in Diversity and Unification

> There are different kinds of gifts, but the same Spirit distributes them . . . Now to each one the manifestation of the Spirit is given for the common good. To one there is given through the Spirit a message of wisdom, to another a message of knowledge by means of the same Spirit, to another faith by the same Spirit, to another gifts of healing by that one Spirit.
>
> *—1 Corinthians 12:4, 7–9*

God has given all of us gifts. When you think about the body, every element is essential and serves a different function: Eyes are for sight, ears for hearing, noses for smelling. Envision this with me for a moment: your hands smelling, your ears tasting, and your nose seeing. Eerie, right? Our body parts know how to operate efficiently, working together, embracing unified capabilities.

There is also purpose in your uniquely handcrafted gift of self. Using the gifts He has instilled within you positions you for your purpose. God does things abundantly, above all that we could ever think of or imagine.

As a writer and therapist, I realize that my writing style and therapeutic approach are different from those of my peers. I bask in my unique gifts, however. I celebrate my individual ways. I also celebrate my peers and honor their originality, because God doesn't require us to execute our gifts the same way. Yet we all have the same purpose: glorifying His name. Honor God with your unique gifts, because there's beauty in diversity and in unification.

REFLECTION

- How are you using your personalized gifts to advance God's Kingdom?

- After reading the analogy of our physical bodies' functions and their importance, what thoughts came to mind?

ACTIVITY

Grab your journal, create a list of your strengths, and develop ten positive affirmations celebrating your uniqueness. Post your affirmations where you can see them, and recite them to yourself daily.

GUIDED PRAYER

Thank You, God, for blessing me with creativity, individuality, and gifts. I honor You and glorify Your name. I love You for molding me as I am fearfully and wonderfully made. Thank You for allowing me to do what I love to serve others. Amen.

Seeing Yourself

But you are a chosen people, a royal priesthood, a holy nation, God's special possession, that you may declare the praises of him who called you out of darkness into his wonderful light.
—*1 Peter 2:9*

Going around the room sharing information about yourself is a piece of cake for some. For others, it is nerve-wracking. At one point, I dreaded the first day of new opportunities, because while it was easy for me to speak of others' accomplishments, I would become tongue-tied talking about myself. What are my hobbies? Goals? What is one cool thing about me?

The more I came to know who I am and Whose I am, however, the anxiety I once experienced began to fade away. I began studying God's Word, asking Him, "How do You see me?" God began showing me who I am by opening doors, using my gifts, and affirming me through His Word. Now I look forward to meeting new people.

We might easily let fear talk us out of oversaturated marketplaces, believing there isn't room for us. God spoke to me, saying, yes, many are authors, therapists, and speakers, but what sets me apart from the rest is the anointing on my life. I stopped shrinking and began using my voice boldly as I engaged with others, knowing that there was no one like me. There is no one like *you*, either.

As you continue to develop spiritually, aligning yourself with God's purpose for your life, you'll begin reframing your thoughts and perceptions about how you see yourself. You are special and chosen.

REFLECTION

- What is the best way to introduce yourself to others? Do you stand boldly in who you are?

- What areas of your life do you need to improve in order to stop shrinking and start standing proudly and securely in your own skin?

ACTIVITY

Draw a circle in the center of a page in your journal. Draw two eyes, a nose, and a mouth inside it. Because this face symbolizes you, be creative. Now, on the outside of your face, write words that describe your identity, in the most positive way you see it.

GUIDED PRAYER

I've been chosen by You, God. I am unique. I am wonderfully made, and I recognize I have been set apart to glorify Your name. I am not perfect, but I strive to let the light within me shine. Amen.

Your Steps Are Ordered

In their hearts humans plan their course, but the Lord establishes their steps.

—Proverbs 16:9

I used to work in a high school's front office. Nicholas, a talented, outgoing, and talkative young man, was one of the students who always found himself in the office to talk with me. Nicholas felt troubled because many in his circle couldn't understand the path he had chosen. His parents had laid out a plan for him to join the military, but he believed God was directing him to use his gifts differently.

Because I knew he was a young man of faith, I reiterated to him, "God has revealed Himself to you in the past. There's no reason to think He won't respond to you now." He considered this for a few days before returning to tell me he felt God had given him the things to say to his parents, and they were now all at ease. Together they mapped out and explored the details of Nicholas's ambition to attend acting and dance school. Nicholas heeded God's voice and is now thriving in his chosen profession.

Reading Nicholas's story may have caused you to remember moments in your life when God led you down a path that others may not have understood. Proverbs 3:5–6 reads, "Trust in the Lord with all your heart and lean not on your own understanding; in all your ways submit to him, and he will make your paths straight." When you submit to God, seeking Him for clarity in the decisions to make, He will guide you, ordering your steps not to lead you astray.

REFLECTION

- Today's devotion focused on trusting God to organize your actions. What crossroad are you presently standing by, trusting God to lead the way?

- As you think back throughout your life, what memories come to you regarding past forks in the road that made you grateful for the journey in the end?

ACTIVITY

Go for a walk or sit outside. Make an intentional effort to notice and appreciate your surroundings. Is this where you expected to be at this point in your life? Even if you didn't feel it, God's hand was guiding you the whole way here. Write down your feelings about where you are right now, literally and figuratively.

GUIDED PRAYER

God, thank You for carrying me when I could not carry myself. Thank You for ordering my steps with grace and mercy. I know You will lead me on. Amen.

Having the Last Laugh

If you are pure and upright, even now he will rouse himself on your behalf and restore you to your prosperous state. Your beginnings will seem humble, so prosperous will your future be.

—*Job 8:6-7*

After searching the internet to find the meaning behind the famous phrase "having the last laugh," I found one in the Merriam-Webster dictionary: "The satisfaction of ultimate triumph or success especially after being scorned or regarded as a failure." I paused for a moment, reflecting on ways your proverbial enemy may have thought he had the last laugh.

However, he didn't know God was in your corner. 1 Peter 5:10 says, "And the God of all grace, who called you to his eternal glory in Christ, after you have suffered a little while, will himself restore you and make you strong, firm and steadfast." Yes, you experienced moments of suffering. Still, God will "restore," which, according to Merriam-Webster, means "to put or bring (something)"— or someone—"back into existence or use."

You may have cried out to God, waiting for Him to answer. But purpose lives *within* you, and you can have the strongest will in existence, because God's spirit dwells there. God will restore you and give you strength, and you will be steadfast and immovable. God purposed you for this journey, and when you arrive at the place destined for you, at that moment, you will look back and be thankful that you didn't give up. With God by your side, you will have the last laugh.

REFLECTION

- What experience have you endured that caused you to become immovable, that you needed faith to see it to fruition?

- What do you feel emotionally, mentally, and spiritually as you remember how you've had that last laugh?

ACTIVITY

Choose a glass or jar—the prettier the better. Take a piece of paper and write down what you are grateful for, each item on a new line. Rip each line from the page, fold it, and place it in your container. Whenever you are so motivated, add strips of gratefulness to that list and jar. Take out your jar or glass and rummage through it whenever you need a gentle reminder of God's goodness.

GUIDED PRAYER

God, thank You for guiding me through my triumphs. Thank You for all the times you restored me and made me strong and steadfast. Amen.

You Are the Shift

The heart of the discerning acquires knowledge, for the ears of the wise seek it out. A gift opens the way and ushers the giver into the presence of the great.
—**Proverbs 18:15–16**

God spoke to me one day when I was praying about an issue I was having, saying, "You are the solution to this situation." I sat with it for a bit before asking God, "If I am the answer, please bless me with wisdom, clarity, and instructions to bring it to fruition." I was struggling with mental health education, stigma, and the junction between psychology and theology. While I witnessed people being prayed for and helped on their path to recovery, it broke my heart to see people turned away because of their condition instead of being covered through prayer.

I sensed there was work to be done. One day, while praying, God revealed to me that He was about to shift me into purpose. God answered my plea by providing insight into how I may integrate spiritual, mental, and emotional intelligence, and wellness education and advocacy, into faith-based groups, government and corporate agencies, and public and private school systems.

Going from a past-focused to a future-focused perspective may be difficult, but keep in mind that you are blessed for the journey. As you shift into purpose, sit at Jesus's feet, praying for wisdom, guidance, and clarity about moving forward, knowing that God will use challenges in our lives to shift our emphasis away from the issue and toward the solution. Remember, you're the shift. We're waiting on you to release your gifts into the world.

REFLECTION

- Have you ever experienced a moment when you felt God gave you a clear answer to a problem you were having? Did the answer surprise you?

- God has used ordinary people to accomplish spectacular and incredible tasks that are mentioned numerous times in the Bible. Can you think of three such stories?

ACTIVITY

Be the shift. Find a way to put something into action today by picking one of the following: volunteering for a new challenge at church, telling someone you are praying for them, or donating your gifts such as art or music to a local school/charity/home for the elderly/needy.

GUIDED PRAYER

God, I am grateful for the gifts You have given me to use for Your glory. As I have been reminded, I am the solution and have the power to change rooms and the nation. Amen.

Rising to the Occasion

For the Spirit God gave us does not make us timid, but gives us power, love and self-discipline.
—*2 Timothy 1:7*

"Rise Up" is a popular song by the American artist Andra Day. It inspires us to persevere in the face of adversity and to be there for others as they face difficulties. It truly captures and represents how I felt in my spirit one day at Barnes & Noble while sitting across from them.

I sat next to her, listening to her tell me about her life. She shared her passion for adolescents and young adults and how this was the time in her life when she could focus on her personal and professional aspirations. She is a married woman with two grown children who has spent her life caring for others. Now she was taking a leap of faith, rising to the challenge, as God aligned her purpose with her time.

She was feeling a lot of excitement and confidence that day, but then fear crept in. "Can I do this?" We can move mountains, as God's power dwells within us. "Being confident of this," Philippians 1:6 says, "that he who began a good work in you will carry it on to completion until the day of Christ Jesus." Walking confidently, several months later, my friend is prospering as a certified life coach, helping youths and young adults.

God offers us a vision, and He will carry it through to completion. You have the power and victory. Now rise to the occasion.

REFLECTION

- When was the last time you had to step up to the plate? What were your emotions: nervous? Afraid? Ecstatic?

- How have Philippians 1:6 and 2 Timothy 1:7 spoken to you today?

ACTIVITY

Write about a time when you needed to take a risk and make a leap of faith. What were your feelings before you leaped, and what happened?

GUIDED PRAYER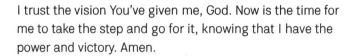

I trust the vision You've given me, God. Now is the time for me to take the step and go for it, knowing that I have the power and victory. Amen.

DAY 30

Relinquishing Control

"For my thoughts are not your thoughts, neither are your ways my ways," declares the Lord. "As the heavens are higher than the earth, so are my ways higher than your ways and my thoughts than your thoughts."
—*Isaiah 55:8–9*

Many people suffer from anxiety when they believe they have little control over the events in their lives, leading to persistent concern. I recently overheard a woman describe her life as rigid. "Uncertainty irritates me. I need to know where everyone is at all times. My calendar must be up to date, I don't welcome change, and I'm in charge of everything in my house."

I pondered her words, thinking, *I wonder what scares her? If she's not involved or does not have complete control, does she fear things falling apart?* Then she walked by me, telling her friend walking alongside her, "It won't get done if I'm not involved!" As a therapist, I routinely teach on this concept, known as "emotional perfectionism." Dr. David M. Burns, a well-known psychiatrist and researcher of depression and anxiety, defines emotional perfectionism as believing you should always feel happy, confident, and in control. I'm here to tell you it is not necessary. Take a breath.

God gave us feelings, emotions, and thoughts, and when you begin to release control and trust the route provided for you, when you open your heart to God's purpose for your life and place your total trust in His plan, you create more moments of tranquility. (It is a lot less draining, too.)

REFLECTION

- Do you find it challenging to maintain control? Do you try to exert control over the course of events?

- How did God speak to you about letting go of control through today's devotion?

ACTIVITY

Make a heart on a page of your journal. In your heart, write down everything you feel you need to control that is better off being surrendered to God. Then look for Bible verses that support your choice to release control of those things, such as Philippians 4:6–7, Isaiah 41:10, and Psalm 55:22. Place your life in God's hands.

GUIDED PRAYER

God, I give up control today, realizing that my ideas are not Yours. Everything, I believe, will fall into place exactly as You planned. Amen.

Finding Purpose in Your Faith

In this third section, you'll find strength, faith, and hope as you continue to develop as a woman of God, learning how your trust and confidence in God correlate with your purpose. Hebrews 11:6 says: "And without faith it is impossible to please God, because anyone who comes to him must believe that he exists and that he rewards those who earnestly seek him." Consider your faith and how it manifests in your life while you read.

Not Needing Your Ducks in a Row

> Then I heard the voice of the Lord saying,
> "Whom shall I send? And who will go for us?"
> And I said, "Here am I. Send me!"
> —*Isaiah 6:8*

The song "Yes" by Shekinah Glory Ministry asks us to consider whether we are willingly and totally pursuing our purpose with our whole hearts, souls, and minds. As I listened, I felt God communicating to me about an opportunity He had placed on my heart at that time. I hadn't moved on it yet because I was afraid, and I was allowing fear to keep me doubtful.

How quickly did I forget my conversation with Monet (see page 38). I thought it was necessary to have all my ducks in a row before walking through the door. I created this checklist in my head, but God showed me that if I trust Him, I must believe that He will dispatch resources and help ensure I have everything I need, just as He did before. But we are human. We all need gentle reminders.

Deuteronomy 31:8 reads: "The Lord himself goes before you and will be with you; he will never leave you nor forsake you. Do not be afraid; do not be discouraged." Here God says He will never leave us, and the glorious part I love about this verse is God going before us. When I gave God my yes by committing to the opportunity and said, "Lord, send me," He did more than I could ever think or imagine. Today, God asks for your yes.

REFLECTION

- Are you presently reviewing all your resources, scared to move because you believe you lack items on your checklist?

- You don't have to have all your ducks in a row, and fear should not keep you stagnant. What has God revealed to you about fear today?

ACTIVITY

Make a line down the middle of a page in your journal. At the top left, write "Fear," and on the right, jot down "Scriptures." Make a list of every fear you have and find scriptures that speak to those fears. Come back and meditate on the scriptures as needed.

GUIDED PRAYER

God, I believe You are dispatching angels to me, providing me with resources as I take this step. I will do what You ask of me as I open my heart to Your will. I believe help is on the way, and You have already gone before me. Thank You, Lord. Amen.

DAY 32

Your Hairs Are Numbered

*Indeed, the very hairs of your head are all numbered.
Don't be afraid; you are worth more than many sparrows.*
—Luke 12:7

I constantly reflect on how I nurture, care for, and provide for my sons. Yes, they are treated the same, but they are individuals. My older son, Bryson, is a more sensitive and empathic child. Braxton is more protective and dominant. I consider how to best care for them as individuals because they each have their own wants, desires, and cares.

I also spend time with each of my sons individually because it's essential in developing our relationships. To honor and recognize my boys' individuality, I customize my time with each one—Braxton enjoys cartoons and is more athletic, so I play soccer with him. Bryson prefers to watch YouTube and enjoys making trendy videos, so with him I commit to learning a new, trendy dance. When together, we watch their favorite shows. God is the same way: He meets us where we are and engages in activities that bring us closer together.

I consider how deeply God understands us, what is hidden in the deep caverns of our hearts, and what is flowing through the subconscious portion of our brains. God knows everything about us, right down to the number of hairs on our heads. The best way to draw out your purpose is going to be different than the way He goes about drawing out mine. Does this imply that we always get it right? No, but God's patience is unrivaled. He knows precisely what you require, when you need it, and when you are ready to accept it.

REFLECTION

- In what ways has God shown up in your life, making you stop and think, *Wow, God, You truly know and understand me?*

- What characteristics of God have you discovered in the way He manifests Himself in Fatherly ways?

ACTIVITY

Show someone you care today by doing something special you know they like. Maybe play their favorite song, cook their favorite meal, or call them and retell a funny story. Let them know you "see" them, you understand them, and they matter to you.

GUIDED PRAYER

God, I am glad You know every strand of hair on my head and every thought I have, and Your love for me is indisputable. Amen.

A Heart of Worship

While he was in Bethany, reclining at the table in the
home of Simon the Leper, a woman came with an alabaster jar of very expensive perfume, made of pure nard.
She broke the jar and poured the perfume on his head.
—**Mark 14:3**

Although the woman with the alabaster jar is unnamed,
her contact with Jesus demonstrates her love, sacrifice,
and devotion in honoring Him. As she breaks the jar,
anointing Jesus with the perfume, the disciples criticize
her behavior. The alabaster jar was a pricey and prized
container, protecting expensive perfume. The disciples felt
she was wasting it.

Then Jesus comes to her defense, saying, "Why are
you bothering her? She has done a beautiful thing to
me." The woman was giving Jesus her very best, and she
was doing so out of pure love, honor, and worship. She
remained unfazed even though everyone else in the room
denounced her decision. I can only imagine how Jesus's
acts must have filled her with love at that moment.

We can learn a lot from the woman with the alabaster
jar, as there are times when others will make snarky remarks
concerning God or His plans. Talking about Jesus can make
others uncomfortable. Allow this woman to encourage you
to focus on Jesus whenever others say negative things
about you or your faith, however. We can see her love for
Jesus in this story, and we can also see Jesus's love for
her in his three words: "Leave her alone." He says that
for us, too. Our sacrifices honor Jesus, as the story of this
woman has demonstrated to us today.

REFLECTION

- How would you describe *your* alabaster jar after reading today's devotion?

- What are some ways you can glorify Jesus by sacrificing?

ACTIVITY

Complete this prompt: "I shall honor Jesus through my . . ."

GUIDED PRAYER

God, it's a privilege to worship and serve You. I praise You for sending Your son, Jesus, and I will worship You in spirit and truth for the rest of my life. Amen.

Broken Crayons Still Color

Three times I pleaded with the Lord to take it away from me. But he said to me, "My grace is sufficient for you, for my power is made perfect in weakness." Therefore I will boast all the more gladly about my weaknesses, so that Christ's power may rest on me. That is why, for Christ's sake, I delight in weaknesses, in insults, in hardships, in persecutions, in difficulties. For when I am weak, then I am strong.

—2 Corinthians 12:8–10

"We are all a little broken. But last time I checked, broken crayons still color the same," said Trent Shelton, a former National Football League player. I was reminded of Shelton's quote while studying 2 Corinthians 12. In this passage, we meet Paul, an apostle who was instrumental in spreading the gospel of Jesus Christ. He's referring to a thorn in his side that he asked God to remove. In verse 9, God responds, "My grace is sufficient for you, for my power is made perfect in weakness."

God revealed to me through the passage that Paul's sense of inadequacy was linked to the thorn, but the thorn did not deter him from fulfilling his purpose on earth because of God's strength. In God's eyes, the grace granted to us gives us the power and strength to achieve our purpose despite the thorn in our side.

God does not require us to be strong in solitude; we are made strong through Him. You have to depend on God, knowing that He'll hold and keep you amid adversity. For this reason, no matter the thorn on your side, God is your strength, and oh yes, broken crayons still color.

REFLECTION

- What have you done with broken crayons to color your life?

- How has God spoken to you today as you consider boasting in your weakness? In what aspects of your life do you currently feel insufficient?

ACTIVITY

Use a broken crayon to draw an image in your journal that represents where you are in life. Would an unbroken crayon have made any difference in the drawing?

GUIDED PRAYER

God, I am thankful today that You're using my imperfections to glorify Your name, fulfilling my purpose. Amen.

Positioned for Overflow

> But Ruth replied, "Don't urge me to leave you
> or to turn back from you. Where you go I will go,
> and where you stay I will stay. Your people will be
> my people and your God my God."
> —*Ruth 1:16*

Ruth and Boaz have a well-known love story in the Bible. Today, I'd like us to focus on Ruth's devoted love for her late first husband's mother, Naomi, and how that dedication positioned her to receive an abundance of blessings.

Naomi's son, Mahlon, married Ruth, a Moabite woman. Naomi wanted Ruth to return home to live with her mother after Mahlon died, as was custom, because Naomi, too, was a widow who had lost both her husband and sons. Ruth was insistent about staying by Naomi's side, however, stating, "Where you go, I will go."

It was a sacrifice because it required Ruth to leave her home and work. Ruth went to work in a grain field to provide for herself and Naomi. As she was working one day, Boaz noticed her and was intrigued. Ruth was intrigued as well, asking Boaz why he showed her favor.

In Ruth 2:12, Boaz replied, saying, "May the Lord repay you for what you have done. May you be richly rewarded by the Lord, the God of Israel, under whose wings you have come to take refuge." Ruth was steadfast, faithful, and unmovable.

Just as the story of Ruth demonstrates the power of love, we must stay the course and remain dedicated to God's plan, for God will do the same for us, positioning us for an overflow of blessings.

REFLECTION

- What has Ruth's story taught you today?

- How has your devotion to God placed you in a position to receive a blessing?

ACTIVITY

Providing for others doesn't always mean in monetary ways. Today, find a way reach out to someone in need. Call someone who lives alone to say hello and listen when they tell you how they are doing. Or hug a friend who is going through a rough time. Or simply say hello to a coworker or neighbor whom no one else talks to. (Maybe you can do all three.)

GUIDED PRAYER

God, I adore You. Thank You for loving me and setting me up for greatness. Amen.

The Advantage of Waiting

For in this hope we were saved. But hope that is seen is no hope at all. Who hopes for what they already have? But if we hope for what we do not yet have, we wait for it patiently.
—Romans 8:24–25

My grandmother and I went shopping for items to decorate my new workplace one day, and we went to a store that sells arts and crafts. As we walked toward the register, my grandmother realized she'd forgotten something. She asked me to wait while she went to find a vase for my office. After a brief wait, she did not return, and a line developed behind me. I looked around from where I was standing, but she was nowhere to be found.

Being impatient, I pulled out my card and paid for the items. My grandmother then stepped behind me and handed the cashier her card. "Ma'am, your granddaughter has already checked out," the cashier said.

"Now, Candace," my grandmother stated, "I told you to wait because I would've blessed you and paid." I recalled a saying: "Just because it is taking time doesn't mean that it won't happen."

Due to my impatience, I didn't follow my grandmother's plea to wait. Sometimes we are impatient with God and try to go ahead of Him. When we can slow down and take heed of His plan, we develop strength in being content while waiting. If you trust what the Lord said, there is an advantage to waiting. God will bless you in ways you can't imagine, just as my grandmother wanted to do for me that day.

REFLECTION

- What have you discovered as your struggle in waiting on God after reading today's devotion?

- Consider a period in your life when you could not wait any longer and decided to go ahead of God. What was the result?

ACTIVITY

Choose an area of your life where patience is required, and write it down in your journal. Then, when God reveals why you needed to wait, return to your journal and write down your views on the significance of waiting for this occurrence to emerge.

GUIDED PRAYER

God, please assist me to be more patient while I wait. I know Your timing is impeccable, yet I require strength to keep from becoming weary. Amen.

Cherishing Every Part of Your Journey

For giving prudence to those who are simple, knowledge and discretion to the young—let the wise listen and add to their learning, and let the discerning get guidance—for understanding proverbs and parables, the sayings and riddles of the wise.
—**Proverbs 1:4–6**

A butterfly's life cycle is divided into four parts. They start as an egg, they become a caterpillar and then a chrysalis, and finally, an adult emerges. From us being in our mothers' wombs to growing into an adult, the stages are parallel. As time goes by, God gives us the ability to manage more, experience more, and fulfill our purpose.

When I look at the stages of a caterpillar's metamorphosis, I see beauty and strength in their transformation. Applying that to our lives, try to appreciate and take pleasure in being the woman of God you are right now while also looking forward to the woman of God you are becoming as you grow spiritually, mentally, and emotionally. Each phase has purpose.

Starting now, begin to cherish every small success, accomplishment, and step along the way. You can undoubtedly discover lessons at every stage of your life if you take a moment to reflect on them, because every encounter, lesson learned, and setback honed your wisdom. It's all preparing you for the journey ahead. No matter where you are on your path, keep the faith. You are going to emerge beautifully!

REFLECTION

- What are you most proud of as a woman at this point in your life?

- How has God prepared you for what He is currently doing in your life, through previous versions of yourself?

ACTIVITY

Find a photo of yourself when you were younger, and write a letter to her. What did you wish someone would have said to her at that point? What do you think future you would tell yourself right now?

GUIDED PRAYER

Thank You, God, for being patient with me and allowing me to grow and develop. I'm grateful for where I'm going while remembering the versions of myself who are no longer with me. I'm excited to grow into a version of myself that's greater than I am now. Amen.

God Will Provide a Way Out

No temptation has overtaken you except what is common to mankind. And God is faithful; he will not let you be tempted beyond what you can bear. But when you are tempted, he will also provide a way out so that you can endure it.

—*1 Corinthians 10:13*

Temptation. We've all experienced being torn between doing what's right and doing what's wrong. If you had a similar upbringing to mine, you might have heard the saying "What is right is right, and what is wrong is wrong. So go ahead and do the right thing." Doing the right thing isn't always easy, though. Some experiences may feel wonderful but are not healthy for us. You may be tempted when you are on track to honor God with your gifts in accomplishing your purpose. It is essential to fight temptation and continue to seek discernment, direction, and wisdom at God's feet.

God will deflect you from going down the wrong path, redirecting you down another, safe one. He will wreck your plans before He allows them to ruin you. And rest assured He will not place more on you than you can handle. Take another look at 1 Corinthians 10:13, and see how it also speaks to God's relentless commitment to saving you. Remember that God knows you, knows what you're capable of, and qualifies and equips you before sending you to fulfill your purpose. Rest assured that He is always with you.

REFLECTION

- How do you define contentment after today's devotion, and how does it appear in your life?

- Do you find it challenging to be content in all situations?

ACTIVITY

Write a letter of gratitude to God.

GUIDED PRAYER

God, I have every reason to trust You because I am confident that You will give me the strength to overcome. Amen.

Seventy Times Seven

*Bear with each other and forgive one another
if any of you has a grievance against someone.
Forgive as the Lord forgave you.*
—*Colossians 3:13*

Ill feelings might occur as a result of holding on to unforgiveness, which can hinder accomplishing your goals. God is asking you to forgive and move forward from the circumstance you are ruminating about right now.

One day, I talked to my mother about forgiveness and how it's not always easy but it is always rewarding. She told me about the several times she had to extend forgiveness because she couldn't bear the anguish if she didn't. For some, forgiveness is difficult because they believe it absolves the offender of responsibility. But moving past it doesn't mean you are telling them what they did is okay. It's releasing yourself from the pain.

God wants us to forgive because it frees us from retaining and hanging on to the suffering. Not forgiving has the power to keep you bound, but as you release and forgive, your health improves, your relationships improve, and you recognize what needs to be mended.

Let's read what Jesus tells us in Matthew 18:21–22: "Then Peter came to Jesus and asked, 'Lord, how many times shall I forgive my brother or sister who sins against me? Up to seven times?' Jesus answered, 'I tell you, not seven times, but seventy-seven times.'" Of course, He isn't saying to count to seventy-seven and then stop; the point is to continue to forgive. No, it's not easy, but it is what God commands us to do—over and over again.

REFLECTION

- How do you define "forgiveness"? Do you find it difficult or natural to forgive others?

- When was the last time you forgave someone for mistreating you? If you are still holding on to the pain, why haven't you let it go?

ACTIVITY

Write about a transgression and include a prayer of forgiveness to the person who mistreated you. Maybe you need to forgive yourself about something. Give yourself permission to be free from that pain—and don't look back.

GUIDED PRAYER

God, I extend forgiveness to others, and I pray that You will give me the strength to let go of the anguish; I don't want to carry it any longer. Amen.

Making Lemonade out of Lemons

I have told you these things, so that in me you may have peace. In this world you will have trouble. But take heart! I have overcome the world.
—John 16:33

I mentor young girls, and during her final year of high school, one of them, Madison, was regularly the victim of cyberbullying from girls at school. It came to the point that she began discussing homeschool options with her parents.

There are college tours, prom, and graduation for students during their senior year of high school, but Madison chose to stay away from those activities. She concentrated on her college essays and asked me to proofread them. Tears welled up in my eyes as I began to read, because she so brilliantly articulated how she was affected by bullying, the steps she had to take to regain her strength in God and His plans for her life, and the process of overcoming a traumatic period in her life.

"Ms. Candace," she exclaimed one day, "I guess some good did come out of a sad scenario because the experience made for an excellent essay, and I learned how to make lemonade out of lemons." Madison's essay exemplified strength, courage, and perseverance in the face of adversity, earning her fifteen college acceptance letters. She learned how to deal with adversity, how God comforts us in our time of need, and how God leads us toward healing to fulfill our purpose.

REFLECTION

- In today's devotion, how did God speak to you?

- What challenges have you faced in your life, and how did you overcome them?

ACTIVITY

For lunch or dinner today, make lemonade or pick through the refrigerator or your pantry to create a new meal. It doesn't have to look perfect or be fancy. Do the best you can with what you have. Surprise yourself!

GUIDED PRAYER

Thank You, God, for defeating the world and residing within me, giving me the same strength to overcome my difficulties. Remind me that I, too, am capable and strong. Amen.

Extending Yourself Grace

But by the grace of God I am what I am, and his grace to me was not without effect. No, I worked harder than all of them—yet not I, but the grace of God that was with me.
—1 Corinthians 15:10

The focus of today's devotion will be on looking within, to discover your strength in extending yourself the same grace and kindness that God extends to us and that you give to others.

You could probably construct an extended list of the many roles you have as a woman. We are all different, from our marital status, education, interests, interpersonal relationships, and employment. Being required to appear in various facets can lead to becoming overworked.

You may feel guilty when tasks are left uncompleted, but give yourself grace. God wants to use you, but He also wants you to relax, and the two can coexist. It is okay to order takeout because you haven't finished your laundry or are too exhausted to prepare a full-course meal. Breathe. Having self-compassion is necessary. Being a stay-at-home mom, a CEO, a yoga instructor, or a college student all have a purpose, and so does taking a break.

Deborah Day, a counselor who helps her clients overcome self-defeating thoughts, feelings, and behaviors, once said, "Lighten up on yourself. No one is perfect. Gently accept your humanness." Before you assume your roles, remember you are a woman first. Your body is in dire need of you. Your mind, like your soul, needs you to be present. You can't be present if you're overworked.

REFLECTION

- How do you communicate to yourself after a mishap or an unfinished task? Do you have self-compassion?

- What are some ways you can be kinder to yourself?

ACTIVITY

When was the last time you made a silly mistake or didn't get something right and called yourself a name for not doing better? Think back to that moment, and talk to yourself in the third person. Tell yourself, *I forgive her.* Remind her she's human and allowed to make mistakes.

GUIDED PRAYER

God, please help me extend more kindness, grace, and compassion to myself. Please help me stop being critical of myself and instead see the strength and beauty in who I am. Amen.

From Existing to Living

There is a time for everything, and a season for every activity under the heavens.

—*Ecclesiastes 3:1*

In Ecclesiastes 3, God tells us there's a time for everything, "a time to tear down and a time to build, a time to weep and a time to laugh, a time to mourn and a time to dance." If you look back over your life, you'll see that there were many different moments that all had a sacred and significant memory or feeling. Surely, some situations in your life rock you to your core and make you feel as if you can't continue. You may be in this space presently.

At times, we can get caught in our grief, but every season brings transformation. I was speaking with a grieving friend who said she felt hopeless and didn't see the purpose in what she was experiencing. She shared, "I want to go from existing to living. I just don't know how to do that." We briefly embraced each other, and as tears streamed down her face, I began praying for her: "God, may you comfort her in this time of sadness, grief, and pain. We don't always comprehend why our loved ones must leave us so quickly. My friend needs a gentle reminder that she still has a purpose, and there is still life after the disappointment. Help her know every experience works for our good."

In the middle of my friend's grief, she found healing, and out of her agony, she founded a new ministry that provides tools and assistance to those grieving. It's therapeutic for her to help others, and it serves as a continual reminder that God is close.

REFLECTION

- Are you mourning the loss of a loved one, or maybe not a physical loss but an unfavorable outcome?

- What do you need at this time in your life to move on from grief or disappointment?

ACTIVITY

Turn on some relaxing music. Feel the sounds; hear the lyrics. Let nothing else matter for a few minutes.

GUIDED PRAYER

God, I pray for comfort, direction, and peace amid loss. Amen.

The Prevailing Purpose

*Many are the plans in a person's heart, but it is the
Lord's purpose that prevails.*
—**Proverbs 19:21**

The book of Proverbs is regarded as the book of wisdom. I am led to Proverbs when I pray for guidance. One day, as I sat at my kitchen table reflecting on my life, the decisions I'd made, the chances I'd had, and the doors closed on me, I was reminded that God's plan had always prevailed and worked out better than I imagined. I reflected on decisions that appeared to be wonderful, but I had to discern if they were from God and whether they were beneficial to me. I had to learn not to allow my excitement to overshadow my judgment, to be slow to respond, and to seek God first.

Even if the opportunities offered to me seem incredible, I have to remember that my thoughts are not His, and that seeking God and waiting for His answer is advantageous. I will go further heeding to His plan than to my own. There will be times in your life when you must seek God and ask, "Is this a good opportunity for me? Should I connect with this person?" Asking does not mean the person is not a good person or the opportunity isn't good; it's seeking wisdom to discern if they are connected to your purpose.

I recall sulking when God told me something wasn't good for me, because I wanted it to be. But after a while, God revealed to me why He said no: It was for my safety. Trust God's no, even when it's hard to hear.

REFLECTION

- Can you think of a time when you were grateful that God intervened in your plans?

- When was the last time you ended a friendship, job, or activity because you heard God telling you it's not good for the path He's set you on?

ACTIVITY

Meditate on Proverbs 19:21, and write down what God says to you concerning your current plans. His response might take a day, week, or month, but it will come to you.

GUIDED PRAYER

God, I surrender my plans to You. Help me seek You and discover Your will before making a decision. Amen.

God Will Handle the Rest

So do not fear, for I am with you; do not be dismayed, for I am your God. I will strengthen you and help you; I will uphold you with my righteous right hand.

—*Isaiah 41:10*

Isaiah 41:10 tells me that God will hold me together in His holy hand despite my worry. I recall being a young single mother, earning my bachelor's degree while working full-time. Even though I was exhausted, I believed that God wanted to do a great work within me, even if all I cared about at the time was survival. I used to cry myself to sleep, unsure of how I'd make it or how life would turn out, but still trusting in God.

When I could have let the weight of the world devour me, God kept me together by placing His angels around me, encouraging and supporting me along the way. Everyone God brings into our lives has a purpose. God used people to help me walk through what could have continued to be an exhausting season in my life. He helped me by turning it around, and it is now a time in my life I am grateful to have experienced because I met some of the most beautiful souls along the way.

Balancing education while caring for your family, working a full-time job, and running a business in your spare time can be difficult. You may feel alone right now and need strength to continue on your road; nevertheless, have faith in God's ability to strengthen you. God will bring the right people and resources into your life to assist you. Consider this today: If you focus on what needs to be done and prioritize God, He will take care of the rest.

REFLECTION

- How did you feel after reading Isaiah 41:10? Did it provide you with peace of mind, comfort, or reassurance?

- As you read today's devotion, did God place someone on your heart who has been encouraging?

ACTIVITY

Spend time with someone today who brings you peace and comfort. Thank them for being there for you and sharing your journey.

GUIDED PRAYER

God, thank You for sustaining me in my time of need and bringing people who care about me into my life. Amen.

Don't Wait to Live

Instead, you ought to say, "If it is the Lord's will, we will live and do this or that."

—James 4:15

One day, I watched a television show and the actress Drew Barrymore was sharing with the audience some of the jewels she learned in life thus far. She stated, "Don't wait to be rescued. Rescue yourself first, and then you can go find anything and do everything and anything." I pondered on her words as I thought about how many of us are waiting to live. As a young girl, you may have dreamed about how you wanted your life to unfold, and you can still desire and seek God on the matter, but you do not have to wait for that dream to come to fruition before going out and living your best life.

Psalm 37:4 says, "Take delight in the Lord, and he will give you the desires of your heart." We all have desires, dreams, and hopes, but we should not put off living until God grants us our heart's desires. We should embrace life as it develops, finding beauty and strength in the things within our grasp.

Yes, seek God and continue to seek Him while still living. Accept where God has you right now, but keep in mind God is omnipotent and omnipresent, so don't get too caught up in rigid plans. He knows the beginning and the end. Remember, everything will work out for your good in the future. Live confidently in the moment. Please embrace life as it is today and find beauty in your surroundings. Don't wait to live.

REFLECTION

- How can you become more present?

- How can you take better advantage of the blessings you have right now?

ACTIVITY

Take a few minutes out of your day to schedule a fun activity with a kind friend that you've been putting off, even if it's a video call where you can enjoy each other's company.

GUIDED PRAYER

God, thank You for knowing what's best. Please help me be more present and focused on recognizing and enjoying where You have me in this moment. Amen.

Walking the Path God Has Laid

In this fourth section, you'll find devotions on following God's path and growing spiritually to come into alignment with your purpose. Psalm 32:8 says, "I will instruct you and teach you in the way you should go; I will counsel you with my loving eye on you." God is the Master in guiding us. Acknowledge Him while you're traveling this path and putting your faith in Him.

No Longer Bound

The Lord said to him, "Who gave human beings their mouths? Who makes them deaf or mute? Who gives them sight or makes them blind? Is it not I, the Lord? Now go: I will help you speak and will teach you what to say."

—*Exodus 4:11–12*

God selected Moses, who had a speech impediment, to lead the Israelites to freedom by parting the Red Sea. Moses shares his shortcomings with God in Exodus 4, explaining why he shouldn't speak on behalf of the people of Israel, but in verse 12, God says, "Now go; I will help you speak and will teach you what to say." Even if you don't have enough, God will provide you with everything you require.

If God has called you to speak, He'll provide you with the words you need. God will provide you with creativity if He asks you to teach. God will present you with a strategy if He wants you to start a business or ministry. When God gives you a big dream, you may look at your bank account and think, *How, God?* I've learned over the years that if it's God's will, He'll pay the bill and qualify the unqualified.

He has many amazing things in store for you to accomplish, and some of them have nothing to do with your public speaking ability, educational background, or financial situation. Whatever God has called you to do, don't focus on your lack; instead, focus on the One who will provide you with all you require. Whatever God has placed within you is linked to souls needing liberation, renewal, and edification. As you journey ahead, remember you serve a God who has no bounds.

REFLECTION

- What did today's devotion teach you?

- Have you ever approached God with Moses's mentality of "how"? How did things unfold?

ACTIVITY

The way God helps might be in the form of local classes being offered (that you need to sign up for) or a friend/colleague with available resources (that you need only ask to use). Look around at, and accept, the ways He is offering you help today.

GUIDED PRAYER

God, remind me that I'm not lacking anything with You, knowing that You will give me strategy and insight, and make provision to carry out what You've placed within me. Amen.

Comfort Zones

I will give you a new heart and put a new spirit in you;
I will remove from you your heart of stone and give you
a heart of flesh. And I will put my Spirit in you and move
you to follow my decrees and be careful to keep my laws.
—**Ezekiel 36:26-27**

We can become conditioned to and complacent in our comfort zones, keeping us stagnant, but seasons change, and we, as women, do as well. Every day, our growth progresses and we discover something new. As a result, you're not the same woman you were the day before. You'll notice that when you spend more time in God's presence, things change. Your mindset, perspective on life, plans, and ideas are infused with His.

For this reason, understand you have the right to change and grow as a woman, daily, to fulfill your purpose. God will sometimes make you uncomfortable in your current situation, to push you to venture outside your comfort zone, to fulfill His will. Some of us align with our purpose due to discomfort and unpleasant situations, but change is good; God has already gone before you if He places you in a new setting.

Isaiah 45:22–23 says, "I will go before you and will level the mountains; I will break down gates of bronze and cut through bars of iron. I will give you hidden treasures, riches stored in secret places, so that you may know that I am the Lord, the God of Israel, who summons you by name." Step bravely outside your comfort zone, knowing that God will take care of the rest when you do.

REFLECTION

- When was the last time God caused you to step outside your comfort zone? How did things turn out?

- Do you believe you have the right to change your mind about anything, even if it goes against the grain or takes you out of your comfort zone to obey God?

ACTIVITY

Look up the Personal Bill of Rights on the internet and reflect on these rights while writing your thoughts in your journal.

GUIDED PRAYER

God, as I walk with You, please grant me strength to venture out of my comfort zone as I find my purpose. Keep me grounded in knowing that You're with me. Amen.

Get into Position

Then he said to her, "Daughter, your faith has
healed you. Go in peace."
—Luke 8:48

There is a story in the Bible about a woman with a medical
condition. Her name is not mentioned, nor is her physical
condition defined. We do know she had this condition for
twelve years. It's presumed she sought medical counsel
from a slew of doctors throughout those years, draining
her savings, and she was exhausted.

Jesus was traveling around the city of Capernaum
with His disciples, casting out demons, healing the sick,
and rescuing the lost. Among this crowd was the woman,
who had entered the gathering by faith. She was part of a
group of people who were also in need of a miracle.

The woman could have allowed her anxiety and fear
to keep her at home, but she was determined to be in
position. She was courageous despite being in pain and
being marked as an outcast. She was tired of suffering
and dealing with the pain, but she exercised her faith to
receive what she was seeking after her healing. Her purpose was to get in the presence of Jesus.

We, too, must rely on faith to get through life. We
must put ourselves in a position where we have faith in
God to do what we cannot do. No matter how many times
you have to start over, keep the faith, release the shame
and guilt you may feel, and get back into position, trusting that Jesus will show up and out, just as He did for the
woman in today's devotion. Your perseverance will bring
you to your purpose.

REFLECTION

- As you read today's devotion, how did God speak to you?

- Was there an instance when your perseverance paid off?

ACTIVITY

List three goals you've been trying hard to accomplish, such as school or relationship change or a nutrition plan. Now pick one, and create a plan to make it happen. Implement one of those steps today. You are in the driver's seat.

GUIDED PRAYER

God, please keep me from getting discouraged when I have to keep trying. Please give me the courage to try again, knowing that you will make it happen when the time is right. Amen.

Leave Empty

For we are God's handiwork, created in Christ Jesus to do good works, which God prepared in advance for us to do.
—Ephesians 2:10

One night while scrolling through Instagram, I came across a post by Maya Elious, a business and branding strategist, that read, "The best way to show God your gratitude is to leverage the gifts he's given you. Dream big. Go after everything that's yours. Leave this world empty." I immediately remembered a conversation I had with a deacon from my church many years ago. He stated, "When I leave here, Candace, I want to know that I poured out everything God poured into me, and I honored God with my time, talents, and gifts."

Colossians 3:23–24 says, "Whatever you do, work at it with all your heart, as working for the Lord, not for human masters, since you know that you will receive an inheritance from the Lord as a reward. It is the Lord Christ you are serving." Make a strategy to pour out everything God has given you. If God has given you the vision to start a business, then start building a business strategy. Start writing the book you've been putting off. Seek out the mentor God has placed on your heart to approach.

The author and motivational speaker Leo Buscaglia once remarked, "Your talent is God's gift to you. What you do with it is your gift back to God." How are you returning God's gift to Him? Are you giving 100 percent, leaving nothing behind? Will you leave this world empty? Today, consider these questions.

REFLECTION

- How has God spoken to you through the devotion today?

- What does dreaming big mean to you?

ACTIVITY

Take out your journal and make a to-do list of your short- and long-term goals. Make check marks next to items that are in God's best interest. Are you giving those your all?

GUIDED PRAYER

God, I pray over my goals, gifts, and abilities today. I surrender them to You, aligning them with Your will and plan for my life. Please assist me in pouring out everything that's inside of me. Amen.

DAY 50

You Are Right On Time

But do not forget this one thing, dear friends: With the Lord a day is like a thousand years, and a thousand years are like a day. The Lord is not slow in keeping his promise, as some understand slowness. Instead he is patient with you, not wanting anyone to perish, but everyone to come to repentance.

—2 Peter 3:8–9

I had a conversation with a woman I met at a conference about God loving us so much that He'll delay answering prayers to prepare us. While we were getting to know each other during a break, she told me, "I compare myself to others often. When I look at their accomplishments, degrees, and lifestyles, I feel I'm behind them. I will be thirty-four years old soon, and I am still working on goals for myself. It is all very depressing."

I then softly spoke to her because I could tell she'd been down about everything for some time: "Do you know when Jesus began His ministry publicly?" She responded, "I do. He was thirty." She didn't say anything else. I didn't say anything else, either. After a pause, I added, "God's delays are sometimes for our benefit, and if God has promised you something, time is irrelevant. God has the power to make it happen at any time." She looked at me and smiled.

God wants the best for us, and He will invest time in our development. It could be the advancement of one's spiritual journey. It could mean preparing you for what you're seeking, emotionally, mentally, or financially. For this reason, embrace God's sovereign love, because you are never late but always on time, as He intended.

REFLECTION

- What have you been asking God for, and do you believe you're ready to care for it if He blesses you today?

- What have you accomplished that others may have thought you were too old or too young to do?

ACTIVITY

As a positive affirmation, write out twenty times: "What God has for me will arrive on time, since His timing is perfect."

GUIDED PRAYER

God, I pray for patience and wisdom today. I will stop comparing my life to others and trust in Your timing, believing that I am on track to receive what I need. Amen.

DAY 51

The Power of Prayer

There was also a prophet, Anna, the daughter of Penuel,
of the tribe of Asher. She was very old; she had lived with
her husband seven years after her marriage.
—**Luke 2:36**

As women of God, we have power, strength, and boldness. When I think about women in the Bible who represent these attributes, Anna comes to mind. Anna was a widow and a prophetess, a female prophet who hears God and represents Him on Earth. Anna is described as "very old" by Luke. Her spirit, on the other hand, was fresh and vivacious. Verse 37 reads, "and then was a widow until she was eighty-four. She never left the temple but worshiped night and day, fasting and praying."

Anna was given the ability by God to break generational curses, release burdens, and lead individuals who had wandered away to seek God. Verse 38 reads, "Coming up to them at that very moment, she gave thanks to God and spoke about the child to all who were looking forward to the redemption of Jerusalem." Like Anna, God will use you to speak up for those who have no voice. He will empower you to stand in the gap for justice, to fast, and to pray in order to move mountains.

The lesson of Anna's prayer life is so important because we can't accomplish our purpose on this earth unless we go to God for wisdom, insight, and guidance. Seek God before each board meeting or consultation call, or first thing in the morning. Anna was focused, committed, and filled with a burning desire to seek God daily; we should desire to be, too.

REFLECTION

- How did God speak to you after reading today's devotion?

- What would you say is the best way to describe your prayer life?

ACTIVITY

Take a walk or spend some time outdoors, seeking God's guidance on ways you can be a role model like Anna, praying for others.

GUIDED PRAYER

God, I thank You for Your presence. Please help me be more deliberate in my prayer and devotion time. Amen.

Glance Up

He gives strength to the weary and increases the
power of the weak. Even youths grow tired and weary,
and young men stumble and fall, but those who hope
in the Lord will renew their strength. They will soar on
wings like eagles; they will run and not grow weary,
they will walk and not be faint.

—*Isaiah 40:29–31*

Some days, you will feel fatigued and wonder, *What is the point?* Regardless of our profession or experience, we all have those times when we wake up and pause to ponder the day ahead.

On those days, it is essential to allow God to renew your strength as you pursue your purpose. Keep in mind that when you're ready to give up, all you have to do is glance up. If God has brought you to this stage in your life, you can rest assured that He'll see you through. According to Psalm 121:1–2, "I lift up my eyes to the mountains—where does my help come from? My help comes from the Lord, the Maker of heaven and earth." Yes, you will feel exhausted and frustrated throughout your life, but you can't forget God is eagerly waiting for you to ask for His help.

I was reminded of a conversation I had with my younger brother while meditating on these verses. He is twenty-six years old and works long days to support himself. He was frustrated, exhausted, and burdened. I shared with him if he kept his eyes fixed on the Lord, God would bless him abundantly. After praying about his circumstances, God gave him insight into a career that would help him make a better living. He glanced up!

REFLECTION

- If God were to call down to you and ask how He can help you, what is the first thing that comes to mind?

- When was the last time you glanced up to ask for personal help, and how did God respond?

ACTIVITY

Make a quick list of ways you'd like God's help today. Then simply glance up and ask.

GUIDED PRAYER

Today, as I look up and see You, God, I thank You for all the times You've helped me soar like an eagle. Please keep me afloat. Amen.

It's All Working for You

Dear friends, do not be surprised at the fiery ordeal
that has come on you to test you, as though something
strange were happening to you. But rejoice inasmuch as
you participate in the sufferings of Christ, so that you
may be overjoyed when his glory is revealed.
—*1 Peter 4:12–13*

Being a woman of God does not make you immune to turbulence, and there are moments in life when you can't comprehend adversity. But God promises He will use our pain for our good. I have experienced my share of difficulties, and as a woman now divorced, I can say God is a promise keeper.

God is molding us into being the women He created us to be. He uses every tear shed. He counts them and uses them to bless us. We serve a strategic and intentional God. Many don't want to experience the crushing and pressing, but just as diamonds are refined under pressure and olives are pressed to produce oil, it's the process that makes room for God's promise.

The familiar story of Jesus raising Lazarus from the dead is a favorite of mine because Jesus wept, knowing what Lazarus had to experience. It had to happen for Jesus to perform the miracle. I believe Jesus weeps with us, but because there's purpose brewing, He knows God is repositioning us. He knows that what's ahead is worth it. God is pruning, molding, and moving to catapult you into purpose. Remember, it's all working for you, working for your good. Today, focus on God's promise and not the process, as one day, you'll look back with gratitude.

REFLECTION

- What thoughts come to your mind as you read Romans 8:28?

- Would life be better if we never faced adversity or felt pain? Why or why not?

ACTIVITY

Grab your journal, write your name in the middle of a page, and underline it. Draw lines from your name, write down difficult situations you are facing, and draw a circle around each one. Pray about those circles.

GUIDED PRAYER

God, I am encouraged today that You are still good in the midst of trials and tribulations. Help me release the burden I am carrying, trusting You are using it for my good and purpose. Amen.

DAY 54

Memories of Yesterday

Forget the former things; do not dwell on the past. See,
I am doing a new thing! Now it springs up; do you not
perceive it? I am making a way in the wilderness and
streams in the wasteland.
—**Isaiah 43:18–19**

Facebook has a daily feature on your timeline called
"Memories." It takes you down memory lane, showing
pictures and posts you made several years ago on that
day. I recall logging into my account one day and seeing
photos from many years before. Usually, I would bypass
the memories, but I paused to reflect.

I thought back to where I was mentally, emotionally, physically, and spiritually that day—a young single
mother who could not possibly imagine how her life would
be unfolding now. I didn't know my purpose, I didn't hang
out at the safest places, and not all my friends had my
best interest at heart. I'm grateful that God intervened
on many occasions to redirect me and the plan I thought
was best didn't come to pass. Still, as I mature spiritually,
I see that God used every good and not-so-good decision
to fulfill my purpose.

The past, at times, will cause you to become impris-
oned, keeping you in bondage due to the mistakes made.
But today God wants you free. For this reason, stay the
course and look forward as God is getting ready to do a
new thing in you. Release ruminating on the past, and
if you're wrestling with shame or guilt, give it to God.
Remember, there's purpose in our story, even if we didn't
know it at the time.

REFLECTION

- What memories of the past keep coming to your mind, and what past mistake do you need to unbind?

- How did God speak to you today regarding your past, and how can you look forward to the future?

ACTIVITY

Take a stroll down memory lane. Pick a photo from Facebook or a photo album and complete this journaling prompt: What was taking place in your life then, and what's one positive thing from the past God is using today to edify yourself and others?

GUIDED PRAYER

God, I am thankful for my past. It has prepared me for the present day. I release the shame and guilt over decisions made in the past, and I'm moving forward with a new mentality trusting in You, Lord, to use my life to glorify Your name. Amen.

DAY 55

Changed Plans

Am I now trying to win the approval of human beings, or of God? Or am I trying to please people? If I were still trying to please people, I would not be a servant of Christ.

—Galatians 1:10

My older son, Bryson, rushed over to me at the kitchen table, eager to share his ideas for celebrating his four-teenth birthday at a restaurant/arcade. He had been talking about his birthday for weeks. He told me what he wanted to wear and who he wanted to invite, and texted me pictures of cakes and decorations. As I was cooking one evening, I overheard him speaking with his friend, Leo, who suggested laser tag as an alternative to the arcade. Bryson abruptly changed his mind and asked me if he could instead go laser tagging.

The next day, before securing the party location, we went to check out laser tagging, and let's just say Bryson was not impressed. Bryson turned to me after viewing the place and said, "Mom, let's stick to the arcade." I started asking him why he had chosen Leo's plan over his own. I gently reminded him, "It's your birthday, not Leo's, baby. Don't be pushed into their agenda, because the point of your birthday is to spend it doing the things *you* want to do." He grinned, we hugged, and he had a great time with his friends and family the following week.

Being God's daughter does not necessarily guarantee that you will fit in. At times, you may feel isolated from the crowd, but you have been chosen, and favor follows you wherever you go. Stick to the plan—God's plan.

REFLECTION

- Describe an instance in your life when you were presented with a different option but chose the original plan.

- Have you ever experienced isolation while following God's plan?

ACTIVITY

Think about your friendships. Do they honor God? Do they make you stray from God's plans? In your journal, make a list of your friends and a brief comment about how each honors God.

GUIDED PRAYER

God, I pray that You will give me wisdom as I discern and navigate friendships. Help me change the ones that don't serve You well. Amen.

DAY 56

Shifting Atmospheres

Then Miriam the prophet, Aaron's sister, took a timbrel
in her hand, and all the women followed her, with
timbrels and dancing. Miriam sang to them: "Sing to the
Lord, for he is highly exalted. Both horse and driver he
has hurled into the sea."
—*Exodus 15:20–21*

Miriam is the first female prophet in the Old Testament, or
a "prophetess" in some translations. God used her to save
her younger brother Moses from Pharaoh as an infant,
when his mother hid him in a basket to protect him. Her
bravery is described in Exodus 2:5–10, but today, let's look
at her acts in Exodus 15.

Verse 19 explains the time the Red Sea was parted
in front of the Israelites, and Pharaoh's army, complete
with horses and chariots, was chasing behind. When God
brought the waters of the sea crashing back over Pharaoh
and his men, Miriam and her Israelites were safe; they
walked through the sea on dry ground.

Miriam trusted God to fix the danger. When He did, she
honored God with praise. Miriam's deed demonstrates that
we should glorify God both during and after the storm.

God may have called you to lead a project, an assign-
ment, or a meeting, and the fact that He has placed you
in the room indicates that you are capable of succeeding.
Learn from Miriam. Don't be intimidated if you're the only
woman in the room. God may have placed you there to
shift the atmosphere. Miriam thrived in the company of
her brethren. Remember you, too, have God's power inside
you, and the Holy Spirit who will guide you.

REFLECTION

- Have you ever been the only woman in a room? How did you feel in such a situation, and did you walk bravely or timidly?

- Have you ever faced discrimination because you are a woman?

ACTIVITY

Find two women in the Bible, along with Miriam, and write what you admire about all three of them in your journal.

GUIDED PRAYER

God, thank You for making me fearfully and wonderfully woman. Please help me embrace the power and anointing I have inside me to shift atmospheres. Amen.

Locating and Heeding to Your Purpose

Commit your way to the Lord; trust in him, and he will do this: He will make your righteous reward shine like the dawn, your vindication like the noonday sun.

—*Psalm 37:5-6*

Sitting on my couch, curled up in the corner, I began studying the Word of God and came upon Psalm 37. I began reflecting on the moments in my life when God's way prevailed over my own, and gratefulness overwhelmed me. The relationships and the opportunities I deemed purposeful weren't, and I had to deal with the aftermath because I did not take a moment to seek God first. Often, we become frustrated in heeding God's purpose for our lives because we are busy figuring it out all on our own. When we commit to God, however, He will reveal His will for our lives, and He will guide and instruct us on the paths to take, causing us to align with our purpose.

In my library, I have a copy of Dr. Tony Evans's Study Bible. Studying Psalm 37:5–6, I read an excerpt of hope inspired by scripture written by Dr. Evans: "Don't worry about locating your purpose if you are seeking God, because your purpose will locate you." The more time you spend seeking God, studying His Word, and committing your way to His, the more the many gifts you have will become apparent and the light you possess will cause purpose to locate and shine upon you just as His word reveals.

As you petition God to reveal His purpose to you, remember to seek Him before you decide to move.

REFLECTION

- Can you think of a time in your life when you were given an opportunity you didn't seek out?

- What is your takeaway from today's devotion, and how will you apply it to your life?

ACTIVITY

Grab your journal, and jot down Matthew 6:33 and Psalm 37:5–6. Meditate on these scriptures and write the words as they enter your spirit as God speaks to you.

GUIDED PRAYER

God, I thank You for sitting with me today. Thank You for shielding, guiding, and redirecting me even when I have followed my way, because I believe that Your way is better. Help me as I move forward, always to seek You first. Amen.

DAY 58

The Power of Godly Voices

*You, however, must teach what is
appropriate to sound doctrine.*

—Titus 2:1

Titus 2 speaks about Godly mentoring. Kindness, self-control, respect, love, and endurance are all mentioned in the text. It also urges individuals who have wisdom to share it with those younger, to help them along their journey.

When I think of Godly leaders, mentors, and advisers, I think of my spiritual mother, Pastor Demery, who walked beside me through my darkest times, when I didn't feel loved, encouraging me, uplifting me, and reminding me of how valuable I am to God. She gave me space to be undone during my divorce and reminded me that I am God's daughter and a force in His Kingdom. She gave me hope when my faith was dwindling. We need Godly voices in our lives; I felt God's love through hers.

I asked Pastor Demery how she uses her God-given abilities to encourage other women not to give up hope and to realize their purpose. "It's a God-given gift to deliver hope to others, and it's an honor to have a gift to aid in activating a different thought process, for people to assist in moving their viewpoint toward hope," she replied.

When you are investing in the lives of others, the goal is to encourage others to build their faith and hope in God, while extending grace and compassion. If, like Pastor Demery, you use your God-given gifts to help other women find their God-given gifts, you double the glorification of God.

REFLECTION

- Is there someone in your life you can turn to as a spiritual advisor? Have you? Why or why not?

- Is there a younger woman in mind whom you could invest in, to help her navigate her life experiences?

ACTIVITY

Write in your journal what you would tell your younger self if you could and one thing you admire about yourself today.

GUIDED PRAYER

God, thank You for the wisdom You've bestowed upon me and for allowing me to pass on the things I've learned through the years to Your daughters. Also, thank You for affirming to me that I'm a valuable asset in Your Kingdom. Amen.

DAY 59

Beauty in Partnership

Two are better than one, because they have a good
return for their labor: If either of them falls down,
one can help the other up. But pity anyone who falls
and has no one to help them up.
—*Ecclesiastes 4:9–10*

Mary, Jesus's mother, was expecting Jesus and had just
been visited by the angel Gabriel, who told her about
God's plan for our Lord and Savior. Mary's pregnancy was
unorthodox. She was pregnant, a virgin, and on the edge
of a scandal, because how could this be?

The angel informed Mary that her cousin, who had
struggled to conceive, was experiencing a miraculous
pregnancy in her older age. Mary and Elizabeth meet in
Luke 1:39–56. Elizabeth encourages Mary and honors her
faith. "Blessed is she who has believed that the Lord would
fulfill his promises to her," Elizabeth says in Luke 1:45.
Exploring their encounter deeper, I tried to envision how
Mary must've felt in this moment, after hearing from Gabriel
and now Elizabeth. They may have hugged deeply, with
warm, happy tears in their eyes.

Mary must have felt so loved by God, as He used
Elizabeth to speak life over her womb, reaffirming to Mary
that she carried greatness inside her. The relationship
between the women grew over these very special miracles
they were experiencing. They had each other to connect
with, since no one else could comprehend the magnitude
of what was going on or validate the wonder of it all.
There is beauty in partnership, and we should all strive to
lift one another up.

REFLECTION

- Did somebody in your circle spring to mind as you read today's devotion? What do you appreciate most about those who are close to you?

- What was your takeaway from Mary and Elizabeth's story?

ACTIVITY

Today, complete an act of kindness to honor a friend who today's devotion reminded you of by sending them a text message telling them how amazing they are, complimenting the qualities you admire, or taking them out to their favorite restaurant.

GUIDED PRAYER

God, I thank You that I do not have to face life alone. Thank You for sending me the people I need to encourage and support me as we fulfill our purpose in one another's lives. Amen.

DAY 60

You Will See Greater Things

Jesus said, "You believe because I told you I saw you under the fig tree. You will see greater things than that."
—**John 1:50**

Yes, we all go through various paths in birthing and discovering our purpose, but the beauty is that we all have the same goal: to use our gifts and calling to glorify God. Our gifts are unique and can be applied in many ways.

Proverbs 4:25–27 reads, "Let your eyes look straight ahead; fix your gaze directly before you. Give careful thought to the paths for your feet and be steadfast in all your ways. Do not turn to the right or the left; keep your foot from evil." The days ahead of you will be far greater than those behind you, as every experience, high, low, success, and lesson learned was designed by God specifically for this season of your life. You are constantly changing and learning new facets of yourself. As you spend time with yourself, soaking in God's presence, remember it is an honor and choice to carve out this time of devotion.

As we mentioned when we discussed the Proverbs 31 woman, you must take care of yourself and not put yourself at the bottom of your list, no matter how full your plate is. Take care of the woman you are now, wave goodbye to the woman you were in the past, and look forward to your future. God already promised you it would be good. Tap into your purpose, passions, and gifts that God has given you, and determine how you might use them to edify the body of Christ and bring glory to God's name. You have so much to offer this world.

REFLECTION

- After reading today's devotion, what was your takeaway?

- What do you hope and pray God will do in your life as you continue to fulfill your purpose?

ACTIVITY

Write a farewell message to the woman you were in the past. Include the ways you are looking forward to your future.

GUIDED PRAYER

God, I'm excited for what's to come. I know I'll see greater things, and I thank You for preparing me to receive and sustain what You have in store for me. Amen.

Continuing Your Faith-Filled Journey

These past sixty days have been filled with praise, joy, and wisdom, as we unpacked, discovered, and rested in your purpose. Thank you for accompanying me on this journey. I'd like to encourage you as you move forward.

As a woman of God, uncovering and implementing various facets of your purpose will be ongoing. It will evolve and change. As you continue to develop your purpose, never forget you are gifted, anointed, and called to greatness. 1 Peter 4:10 says, "Each of you should use whatever gift you have received to serve others, as faithful stewards of God's grace in its various forms."

Keep evolving and intentionally creating time with God. You'll need to be fed by His Word for the path ahead of you. Continue to be the remarkable woman you are, going boldly and courageously after everything God has placed inside you. You are amazing!

Index

ABOUT THE AUTHOR

CANDACE WRITES is the author of *Breathe: Rest, Reflect, Reset.* She is a minister, therapist, and licensed social worker who lives in the metropolitan Washington, D.C., area with her two active sons, Bryson and Braxton. She currently serves in several capacities at Christ Way Cathedral under the leadership of Bishop Ronald and Pastor LaShawn Demery. She is active in the unscripted youth and young adult, and mental health, ministries. Connect with her at Candace-Writes.com.